WORLD

AND AUXILIARY STEAM POWER

g strength and direction of the Winds, and the power of the Vessel.

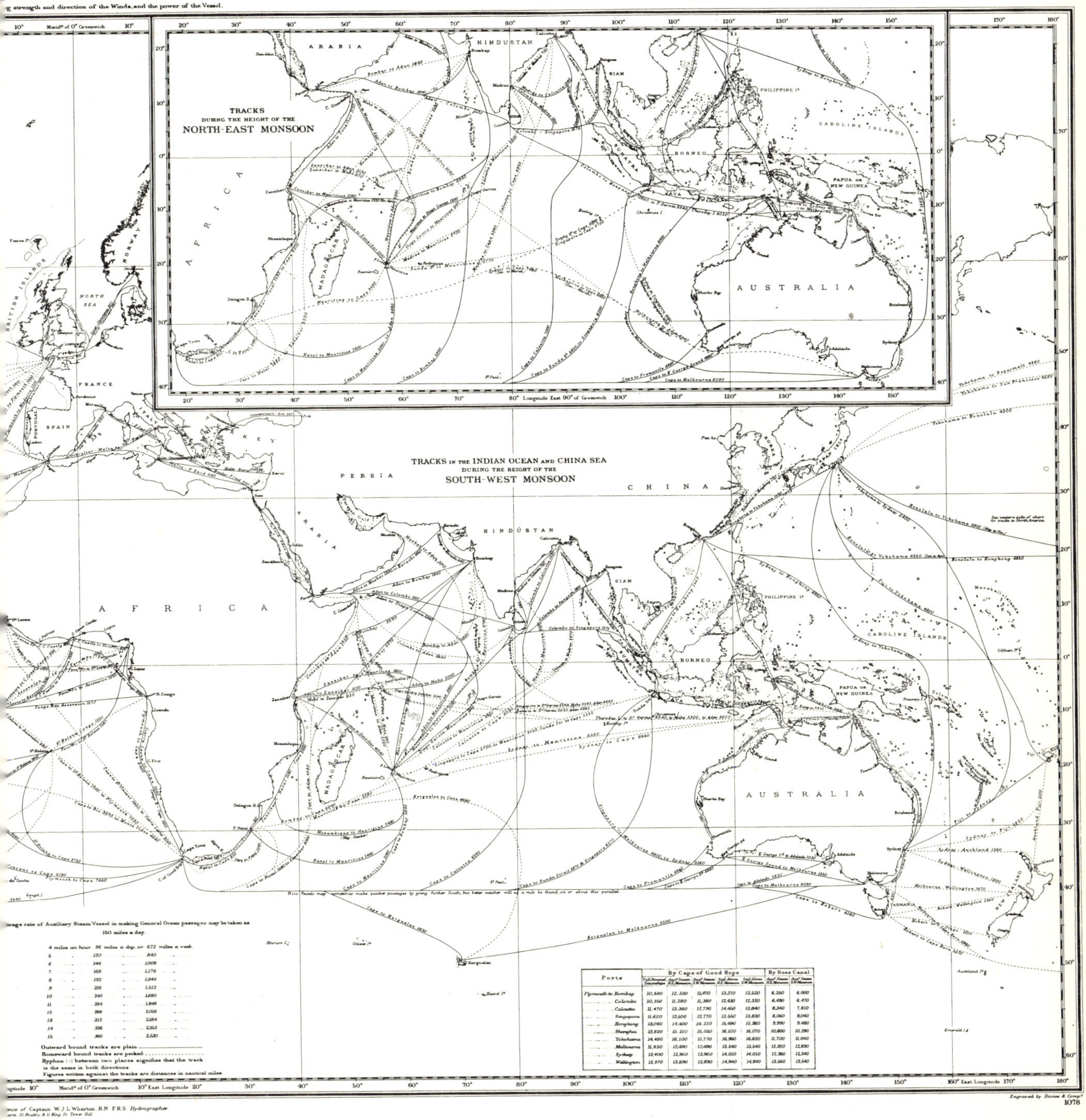

TRACKS
DURING THE HEIGHT OF THE
NORTH-EAST MONSOON

TRACKS IN THE INDIAN OCEAN AND CHINA SEA
DURING THE HEIGHT OF THE
SOUTH-WEST MONSOON

Average rate of Auxiliary Steam Vessel in making General Ocean passages may be taken as
150 miles a day.

4 miles an hour	96 miles a day	or 672 miles a week
5	120	840
6	144	1,008
7	168	1,176
8	192	1,344
9	216	1,512
10	240	1,680
11	264	1,848
12	288	2,016
13	312	2,184
14	336	2,352
15	360	2,520

Outward bound tracks are plain ————
Homeward bound tracks are picked ....
Hyphen (-) between two places signifies that the track
is the same in both directions.
Figures written against the tracks are distances in nautical miles

Ports	By Cape of Good Hope				By Suez Canal	
Plymouth to Bombay	10,890	12,320	11,470	13,270	12,520	6,250	6,000
Colombo	10,350	11,580	11,390	12,420	12,330	6,490	6,470
Calcutta	11,470	13,360	12,770	14,460	13,840	8,240	7,810
Singapore	11,620	12,600	12,770	13,550	13,830	8,060	8,040
Hongkong	13,060	14,400	14,210	15,490	15,360	9,990	9,480
Shanghai	13,820	15,310	15,100	16,370	16,070	10,800	10,290
Yokohama	14,490	16,100	15,710	16,960	16,820	11,700	11,040
Melbourne	11,930	12,490	12,490	13,540	13,540	12,810	12,890
Sydney	12,400	12,960	12,960	14,010	14,010	13,360	13,340
Wellington	12,970	13,890	13,890	14,940	14,940	13,560	13,540

ence of Captain W.J.L.Wharton. R.N. F.R.S. Hydrographer
arts 31 Poultry & 11 King St Tower Hill

Engraved by Davies & Comp.
1078

The Sailing Ships of The New Zealand
Shipping Company, 1873-1900

I. *Rangitiki*, oil painting by F. Tudgay, 1895. (London Office)

The Sailing Ships of The New Zealand Shipping Company, 1873-1900

Alan Bott MA, FSA

(a Director of the Company)

B. T. Batsford Ltd London

To my Family

First published 1972
© Alan Bott 1972
Made and printed in Great Britain by
William Clowes & Sons, Limited
London, Beccles and Colchester
for the publishers B. T. Batsford Ltd
4 Fitzhardinge Street, London W1H 0AH

ISBN 0 7134 0467 1

Table of Contents

Foundation of The N.Z.S. Co. and the first charters, p. 11 – the first owned sailing ships, p. 13 – new tonnage, Blumer's of Sunderland, p. 20 – organisation in New Zealand and London, p. 21 – further new tonnage, Palmer's of Newcastle, p. 24 – competition and freights, p. 25 – the last new building, Stephen's of Glasgow, p. 27 – establishment of the cadet scheme, p. 28 – refrigeration and steam, p. 29 – finance and the transfer of control to London, p. 33 – the Chairmen 1873–1900, p. 38 – the last days of sail, p. 43.

The Sailing Ships

List of Illustrations

Foreword

by F. W. Spite, formerly a Managing Director in New Zealand and in London

It is fitting, on marking The New Zealand Shipping Company's approaching centennial, to produce as complete a record as possible of the company's sailing ships, and I feel privileged to associate myself with Alan Bott's splendid effort in this direction. Theirs was a proud record as a result of being well found and run under strict discipline.

Thanks to Sir Murray Stephen (on the launch of the present *Piako*) my wife has a beautiful reproduction of Spurling's painting of the sailing ship *Piako* (1876), and I may perhaps comment that after I bought Dixon's painting, 'When Sail beat Steam', I had many visits from Captain d'Arcy Maxwell whose view it was that Dixon's version was 'truer to life' than Mason's.[1]

My own service does not go back to the sailing ship days, but I knew their remaining Masters in steam and, in addition, I was fortunate in that my personal friendship with Captain John Bone led to his taking me to dine with Captain H. E. Greenstreet at the old Holborn Restaurant in London in 1925. Previously, a luncheon had been held in Wellington aboard RMS *Remuera* (Captain J. J. Cameron, RNR) in honour of Captain Bone and it was attended by His Excellency the Governor-General, Admiral Lord Jellicoe, as a mark of respect not only for the Merchant Service in general but also for The New Zealand Shipping Company and Captain Bone in particular.

Perusal of the old press cuttings certainly discloses that no other line's vessels, sailing out of the port of London, surpassed the standard set and maintained by the sailing ships of The New Zealand Shipping Company, and the company undoubtedly gained by sea and shore staff subsequently being brought up in this tradition.

Wellington

[1] v. Plates VI, VII and VIII.

Preface

Much of the material for this book has already appeared in the form of articles in *Crossed Flags*, the house journal of The New Zealand Shipping Company, vol. 1, numbers 1–9. Such research as was necessary to establish the history of the sailing ships was done largely during a stay of almost a year in New Zealand on the company's business. In this connection, I wish to acknowledge, with gratitude, the encouragement and advice of two of the company's former Managing Directors in New Zealand, Mr F. W. Spite and Mr T. S. Marchington. To the former I am especially indebted for consenting to write the Foreword. I have also received much help and guidance from a great many other friends within the company, both here and in New Zealand.

In the Introduction, an attempt has been made to outline the company's history in the age of sail, concentrating more particularly on such subjects as have not been dealt with extensively in print elsewhere. The main part of the book deals with each of the sailing ships separately, first setting out their main specifications and then describing the principal events in their history.

The primary sources for this study are the minutes of Board meetings preserved respectively in Wellington and in London. The reports of the Annual General Meetings of the company provide a useful chronicle of the major events of the period. Unless otherwise stated, all quotations in the Introduction are from these sources. Some interesting reports by the ships' surgeon-superintendents on the condition of immigrants and the troubles of the outward voyage are to be found in the New Zealand National Archives. Further, the very full collection of newspapers in the Parliamentary Library in Wellington gives valuable, and often very colourful, accounts of experiences at sea. Lloyd's Register of Shipping has provided the basic data on the ships. There is also, of course, the company's official history *Clipper Ship to Motor Liner* by Sydney D. Waters (London, 1939). In spite of some inaccuracies, *White Wings, Fifty Years of Sail in the New Zealand Trade* by Henry Brett (Auckland, 1924) provides a most useful record of the voyages of the sailing ships. I have used this work generally as a point of departure in the accounts of the ships, illustrating the more interesting or dramatic incidents with corroborative material from the contemporary newspapers. Unless otherwise acknowledged, quotations given on the ships themselves are from *White Wings*. The collections of the Christchurch Museum have provided much useful material for the Canterbury background of the company.

I am grateful to the publishers of the *New Zealand Guide* and *A Dictionary of Maori Place Names* for permission to quote from these works in the account of the derivations of the names of the company's ships which forms Appendix 2. My thanks are also due to the Derby Pure Ice and Cold Storage Co. Ltd. for providing me with the material on *Mataura* and her Haslam patent dry air refrigerator; this is printed in Appendix 3. I am most grateful to Mr John Ellis for allowing me access to his father's papers, which describe so vividly life on board a sailing ship in the 1880s. These have been collated by the latter's grandson, Mr Edward Ellis, and extracts from them are printed in Appendix 4.

Both oil and water-colour paintings exist of many of the 18 sailing ships owned by the company; many of these hang in the offices in London and throughout New Zealand. Fortunately, however, photographs exist of all the sailing ships owned by the company. The Library of the National Maritime Museum at Greenwich contains photographs of almost all the company's sailing ships. But perhaps the finest collection of pictures of the early clipper ships employed in the South Seas is that of the Alexander Turnbull Library in Wellington. I am indebted to the Librarians of both these institutions for permission to reproduce some of these photographs as illustrations. I am also grateful to H.M. Stationery Office and the Hydrographer of the Navy for permission to reproduce the chart shown on the endpapers.

Finally, my grateful thanks are due to Mr and Mrs G. H. Williams for offering some useful criticisms on the book whilst in manuscript as well as giving great assistance with the proofs, also to Mrs Rebecca Doyle for preparing both the typescript and the index.

London, September, 1971   A.J.B.

Introduction

'At a meeting of gentlemen interested in establishing a new line of
ships between London and New Zealand . . .' So run the minutes
of a meeting held in Christchurch on 20 November 1872, when it
was decided that 'it is desirable with the view of providing increased
shipping facilities for New Zealand trade to form a colonial shipping
company'. The particular ends in view were the 'conveyance of . . .
emigrants and cargo'. In January 1873, The New Zealand Shipping
Co. Ltd. was registered and it was immediately decided that an agent,
Mr C. W. Turner of Christchurch, should be sent to England to
arrange matters, and especially 'to tender for the carriage of emigrants' – at £15 per head with discretion down to £14 5s od.

For some time, allegations about the imperfections of the service
offered by the established British lines, Shaw Savill and Co. and the
Albion Line, together with a vigorous spirit of colonial indepen-
dence had inspired the merchants in Auckland, Wellington, Christchurch and Dunedin, the four main centres, to consider the founding
of separate provincial shipping lines. In the middle of 1872, in Auckland, the New Zealand Freight Company had been registered, being
financed by the Bank of New Zealand. It was the initiative of the
local manager of the same bank, J. L. Coster, which led to the meeting in Christchurch four months later and the foundation of The
N.Z.S. Co.[1] The similar financial backing of the two ventures made
an amalgamation of interests possible. The choice of Christchurch,
rather than Auckland, as the centre for what was to be a national enterprise is explained by the primacy of the South Island as the chief
exporter at the time of the major items, wool and grain. Dunedin,
with its staunch Glasgow connections, and served as it was by the
Albion Line, had less sympathy with the London trade, which it
was The N.Z.S. Co.'s mission to serve.[2] By June 1873, the Chairman

---

[1] v. p. 39 and also *White Wings*, p. 250. In the list of the company's original promoters (v. pp. 14–15) the New Zealand Loan and Mercantile Agency Company, an
associate of the Bank of New Zealand, is shown as having 1,000 of the 3,200 shares.
[2] A company called the Otago Freight Association existed in Dunedin – its

1. John Lewis Coster, principal founder of The N.Z.S. Co. and first Chairman of the New Zealand Board, 1873–1874, and again Chairman, 1875–1886. (Christchurch Boardroom)

could claim at a general meeting in Christchurch that 'from all parts of the colony [we are] receiving most encouraging promises of support, particularly from Wellington and Dunedin . . . the public there generally taking a warm interest in the company, considering it in the light of a national undertaking'.[1]

At the same meeting, it was reported that the *Punjaub*, a charter and the first ship in which the company had an interest, had set sail for New Zealand. She was a barque of 883 gross tons which had been built in 1862 by Richardson's of Stockton and was owned by Knevitt and Co. She was just over 180 feet in length and had a beam of a little over 30 feet. The company's first voyage could scarcely be described as an unqualified success. The *Punjaub* had sailed from Gravesend with 340 souls aboard, but, according to *The Lyttelton Times* (22 September), 'during the voyage the deaths had been Danish 21, British 7, adults 8 and children 20. The deaths had resulted from measles 13; teething 4; typhus fever and other causes 11'. A further eight people succumbed shortly after arrival. Subsequent editions of *The Lyttelton Times* give an account of the *Punjaub* – 'she is a fine iron ship . . . a splendid model of a first class clipper . . . with a fine entrance and beautiful run'. The story is completed in the edition of 27 October – 'the light portion of the cargo was discharged with great celerity; all the case and light goods being discharged in four days in excellent order reflecting great credit on those engaged in the work. The first clip of the season will be sent by this vessel.'

In all, 1873 saw an immense amount of activity by the new company. In August, it was resolved by the Board in New Zealand that the

The first owned sailing ships

Chairman was Evan Prosser. This company had already been absorbed by The N.Z.S. Co. by 20 June 1873 (v. note 1 *infra*).

[1] The company's Articles of Association were amended by a special resolution at this meeting in Christchurch on 20 June 1873. This authorised 'the formation of local Boards or Boards of Advice in London and in all or any of the several Provinces of New Zealand'. The provision of representation of the company's interests throughout New Zealand of course helped to foster the idea of a national undertaking. The local Boards were, for many years, each represented on the general Board in Christchurch by at least one member. The original representatives were John Johnston (Wellington), Evan Prosser (Dunedin) and Dr (later Sir) J. Logan Campbell (Auckland). The last named was the first Chairman of the New Zealand Freight Company, and was to remain on the Board of The N.Z.S. Co. until 1889.

At a Meeting of Gentlemen interested in establishing a new line of Ships between London & New Zealand, held in Christchurch at the Offices of the New Zealand Loan & Mercantile Agency Company 20th November 1872 there were present:

Messrs G Gould W Reeves W Montgomery C W Turner J L Coster, A C Wilson, J T Peacock, J Anderson and J Studholme

Mr Coster was voted to the chair

Mr A C Wilson acted as Honorary Secretary

The following list of Promoters ~was~ representing 3200 Shares was read by the Chairman

New Zealand Loan & M A Coy	1000
George Gould	500
R H Rhodes	200
A McLean	200
Studholme Bros	200
C W. Turner	200
W Montgomery	100
John Anderson	100
J L Coster	100
Josiah Birch	100
R Cobb	100
J S Williams	100
Wilson Sawtell & Co	100
W Reeves	100
J T Peacock	100

II. *Rakaia*, the first ship to be built for the company; water colour by J. Forster, 1879. (In the author's possession)

The Chairman addressed the Meeting pointing out the necessity of an independent and colonial line of vessels to trade between New Zealand and London, that the contract between the Government and Shaw Savill & Co. would expire in March 1873 and that after that the Government would be in a position to treat with any ship-owners or Brokers other than Shaw Savill & Co. for the conveyance of their emigrants & cargo.

Outward Freight from London to the Colony was much to be desired and considerable support had already been promised by Canterbury Importers

He was sanguine that if all worked together a powerful line might be established notwithstanding the difficulties that were supposed to exist

Moved by Mr Gould
seconded by Mr Peacock

That it is desirable with the view of providing increased Shipping facilities for New Zealand Trade to form a Colonial Shipping Company with the registered office in Christchurch, New Zealand, the title of the Company to be "The New Zealand Shipping Company Limited and the Capital to be £100,000 in 10000 shares of £10 each

Carried unanimously

The draft Memorandum of Association was then read and paragraphs numbers 1.2.3 (a) (b) (c) (d) (e) (f) (g) 4 & 5 were carried and passed

2. The first two pages of the New Zealand Board minutes, 20 November 1872, when it was decided to form 'The New Zealand Shipping Company Limited'. (Wellington Office)

3. Hereford Street, Christchurch, *circa* 1880. No. 159, the building with the flag-pole, was the company's first office in New Zealand. The building still stands, although the company is now on the other side of the street, at No. 149. (Canterbury Museum)

4. Lyttelton Harbour in the heyday of sail. The company's office is the white building adjoining the store on the extreme right of the photograph. It has three windows on the ground floor and four in the upper storey. (Turnbull Library)

company should 'be represented in London by someone capable of coping with difficulties which would have to be met there during the next two or three years'. In October, three more charters, *Adamant*, *Columbus* and *Hope*, are mentioned. Then in November, the Board minutes reveal that the company 'had chartered 18 and purchased two vessels, the *Hindistan* (*sic*) and *Dunfillan*, both very high class iron ships' and later to be renamed *Waitara* and *Mataura*, and that a 'contract had been entered into for building two 1,000 ton iron ships which were to be launched during the present month and would be named after the rivers Waikato and Waitangi'. In fact, the first ship built for the company was to be called *Rakaia*. Perhaps it was decided more appropriate to use a South Island name for a company founded in Canterbury. Without doubt, the mainspring for all the progress achieved in London during 1873 – the leasing of premises, the chartering and purchasing of ships – was 'the skill and energy and pluck' of Charles Wesley Turner, the company's agent there.

At the first Annual General Meeting of the company, held at the Crystal Palace Music Hall, Christchurch, on 24 January 1874, the Chairman reported: 'A recent cablegram states that Mr Turner has purchased two other ships – the *Scimitar*, of 1,200 tons, and one, the name of which I am sorry to say we cannot make out owing to the difficulty of deciphering the cablegram.' The mutilated name was, in fact, *Dorette*, a ship whose name was to be changed under the company's flag to *Waimea*. *Scimitar* was an auspicious acquisition, for under new ownership she was to bear what became the company's favourite and most famous name – *Rangitiki*.

In proposing the adoption of the report and accounts at the same meeting, Mr George Gould[1] claimed, 'We may fairly congratulate ourselves upon the successful launching of the company. I think that, for a colonial company, it has been one of the most successful schemes that has ever yet been launched in New Zealand.' The congratulations of 1874 were well justified, for the Chairman had just reported that 'the company has despatched no less than 37 ships of very large tonnage from the United Kingdom to the colony, loaded with valuable cargoes; that it has sent six laden vessels from the colony, and there are six more at present on the berth loading for London'. Nevertheless, the Chairman added, 'the company has laboured under

[1] His grandson is the Chairman of the present New Zealand Board.

NEW ZEALAND SHIPPING COMPANY.

---◆---

LONDON OFFICES.................INDIA HOUSE, ALDERMAN'S WALK.

COLONIAL OFFICES.....................................AT ALL THE NEW ZEALAND PORTS.

OTAGO OFFICES.....................HIGH STREET, DUNEDIN.

---◆---

SIR,—

Your attention is respectfully directed to the accompanying advertisement. The NEW ZEALAND SHIPPING COMPANY (LIMITED) is a purely Colonial Undertaking, the whole of the Shares being owned in New Zealand; and, as it is not desirable that the Carrying Trade of New Zealand should be in the hands of Foreign Companies, it is hoped you will give directions to have your Wool and other Produce shipped by the Company's vessels, and will use your influence in its favor. The vessels employed are all of a very high class, and the rates of freight will be kept as low as possible.

I am, Sir,

Yours faithfully,

....

Chairman Local Board.

DUNEDIN,

—————————— 187

NEW ZEALAND SHIPPING COMPANY, LIMITED.

THE following and other high-classed Clipper Ships, owned and chartered by the Company, have been carefully selected on account of their sailing qualities and fitness for the carriage of Passengers, Wool, and General Cargo.   They will be periodically despatched from London for the various New Zealand Ports, and also from all the New Zealand Ports for London :—

	TONS.		TONS.
COLUMBUS	744	SALISBURY	1113
PUNJAUB	883	QUEEN OF THE NORTH	825
ADAMANT	815	W. E. GLADSTONE	534
CARDIGAN CASTLE	1200	HINDOOSTAN	833
CALLER-OU	674	ISLES OF THE SOUTH	821
DUKE OF EDINBURGH	1075	QUEEN OF THE AGE	757
ELIZABETH GRAHAM	589	DUNFILLAN	853
STAR OF INDIA	1045	CARNATIC	871
SURAT	1000	DILHARRIE	1293

5. Two advertisements for The N.Z.S. Co., 1873. *Punjaub,* a charter, was the first ship in which the company had an interest. *Hindoostan* (*sic*) and *Dunfillan* were to become *Waitara* and *Mataura*. The figures given are net registered tons. (London Office)

6. Charles Wesley Turner, a Director on the New Zealand Board, 1875–1880. As the company's first agent in London, he acquired in 1873 the first offices, chartered 37 ships and purchased 4 others. (Canterbury Museum)

7. William Reeves, second Chairman of the New Zealand Board, 1874–1875. (Christchurch Boardroom)

a great disadvantage from the fact that it has had to charter a large number of vessels at a very short notice ... and the real and only lasting cure is for the company to become possessors of its own vessels'.

New tonnage – Blumer's of Sunderland

An initial building programme had been outlined, in fact, at a special general meeting of shareholders at Warner's Hotel, Christchurch, on 1 November 1873. The Chairman had announced that the company had 'contracted with eminent builders at Sunderland, Messrs Blumer and Co., for the building of two 1,000 ton iron ships, complete in every respect and of the highest class'. The two ships mentioned, the first to be built specifically for the company, were to be named *Rakaia* and *Waikato* after major rivers in the two islands – continuing the practice already adopted.[1] The local newspapers of the day succeeded in misreporting the event, describing the builders as 'Messrs Bloomer'! Two months later, at the Annual General Meeting, the Chairman noted that the new ships 'will be turned out completely ready for service at a very reasonable price'. In fact, they cost about £14,000 each, which compared favourably with *Rangitiki*, the most expensive of all the sailing ships ever owned by the company, which had cost £25,000. By the end of the year two further ships from the same yard, *Waitangi* and *Waimate*, had also been delivered. These were a little larger than their two predecessors and cost a little over £20,000 each.

The affairs of the company in the first years were 'conducted very satisfactorily by local boards' at each of the four main ports, with the headquarters, of course, at Christchurch. The Directors all acted in an honorary capacity![2] On 19 May 1874, the 'London Board of Advice' met for the first time, under the chairmanship of J. L. Coster, the Chairman of the New Zealand Board, who remained in London for a few months to see to the formal establishment of the company there. An account was opened – it still remains – with the National Provincial Bank. The London Board's powers included 'the employment and general management of the company's own fleet and

Organisation in New Zealand and London

[1] The sailing ships are here generally considered in the order of their commissioning under The N.Z.S. Co.'s flag. This procedure has seemed more logical than to give precedence, say, to a ship on the date when an order for her construction was given to the builders, over some other ship bought a month later from another owner and ready for immediate service. It may be noted, therefore, that the chronological order of the first eight ships owned by the company adopted here – *Waitara* (September 1873); *Mataura* (October); *Rangitiki* (December); *Waimea* (January 1874); *Rakaia* (February); *Waikato* (March); *Waitangi* (August); and *Waimate* (October) – differs considerably from the somewhat random order of precedence given in *Clipper Ship to Motor Liner*, where *Rangitiki* heads the list. (The months shown are those of outward loading on the first voyage for the company.)

[2] The establishment and purpose of these boards is further discussed on p. 13, note 1.

the provisioning and fitting' of charters, but all its powers were to be 'subject to the directions . . . of the Board in the Colony'. By the end of the year, the London Office had outgrown its accommodation in India House, Alderman's Walk, Bishopsgate, and premises were taken at 84 Bishopsgate. Nine years later, in 1883, when the company had just completed its first decade, the move was made to 138 Leadenhall Street.[1]

In London the new building programme, which had been launched at Blumer's Sunderland yard, involved the appointment of the company's first Superintendent, or Overlooker as he was styled initially. After a careful scrutiny of his five references, Captain Hodgson was appointed Superintendent in 1875 at a salary of £20 per month 'upon the understanding that he devoted the whole of his time to the company's work'. It was also decided that 'a book should be kept to contain a record of Captains' and Officers' antecedents and of their services whilst in the employ of the company'. A year later, the salaries of both the Superintendent and of Captains stood at £25 per month. From the many applications 'to enter the service of the company', the Chairman informed shareholders, it could be seen that 'they were not thought such a mushroom Company after all'. Fifteen years later, the Marine Superintendent's salary had been raised to £400 per annum, while the Superintending Engineer's stood at £200. The Assistant Manager in London received £500, a junior clerk £25 per annum!

In 1875, the London Board of Advice had given thought to the adoption of distinctive livery for the fleet;[2] on 10 August it was recommended 'that all the company's ships be painted black with white ports, masts and yards, etc., of an uniform colour, boats white'. These colours were, of course, continued with the steam ships, and only recently – some 90 years after their first adoption – have there been signs of a new departure in the company's livery, with the two tones of green for the hulls of the six new ships built since 1966.

In retrospect, the achievement of the company in these first two or

---

[1] Rochester Buildings (138 Leadenhall Street) was pulled down in 1964; the company's head office is still on the same site, however, in the new P & O Building.

[2] It is said that the company's original flag consisted of 'a white sheet with the letters "N.Z." over "S.Co." in blue' (*White Wings*, p. 251). No official record appears to exist dating the addition of the St George's cross; a photograph of *Waimate* dated 27 October 1874, however, shows the company's flag as it is today (v. p. 70).

SOUTH WEST INDIA DOCK. WESTERN ENTRANCE.

BARGES WAITING TO LEAVE THE DOCK. *See p. 65.*

8. South West India Dock, western entrance in 1877. This dock was frequently used by the company's ships. (Lithograph from *The Thames and Its Docks* by Alexander Forrow, London, 1877)

three years is amazing. In 1875, a total of 140 ships was despatched from England to New Zealand; of these The N.Z.S. Co. provided 54. Homewards, the company provided over half the total sailings – 25 out of 49. In a comparable period in 1876, The N.Z.S. Co.'s contribution was 53 out and 31 home; in 1877 it had risen to 63 out and 37 home – the bulk of the northbound cargo consisting of 92,652 bales of wool and 10,700 tons of wheat. Doubtless a clue to the reasons for this quick progress is to be found in a circular issued to Otago wool shippers of the time. This advertisement announced that The N.Z.S.

Co. 'is a purely colonial undertaking, the whole of the shares being owned in New Zealand; and, as it is not desirable that the carrying trade of New Zealand should be in the hands of foreign companies, it is hoped you will give directions to have your wool and other produce shipped by the company's vessels'.[1]

The 1870s also witnessed the great boom in emigration. Between the years 1877 and 1882 inclusive, when the company was under contract with the New Zealand government to carry emigrants, it is claimed that The N.Z.S. Co.'s monthly sailing vessels carried nearly 20,000 passengers to New Zealand.[2] In 1875, the peak year for the arrival of new settlers, the company was responsible for nearly 11,500 outward passengers. Inevitably, passengers became an anachronism in the sailing ships long before cargo did so, and the prospect of a quicker passage had, by the early 1890s, diverted nearly all passengers to the steamers.[3] Indeed, by 1888, a *Handbook of Information* for passengers issued by the company for both steam and sailing ships was pointing out the virtues of the *longer* passages afforded by the latter. 'The sailing ships are all built of iron and are of the highest class at Lloyd's. Most of them are full pooped ships with commodious saloons, suitable for passengers seeking a long sea voyage for restoration of health.'

Further new tonnage – Palmer's of Newcastle

In spite of the fact that there was an amount of £14,360 3s 11d standing 'at debit of profit and loss from the commencement of the company to date, after defraying all losses, cost of management, interest, preliminary and special charges and expenses of every kind', the Chairman told the second Annual General Meeting, convened at 'Mr Charles Clark's auction rooms' in January 1875, 'we have already a fleet of eight magnificent ships . . . but the Directors by no means intend to stop here'. Further, 'they have recently entered into arrangements of a most satisfactory nature by which they will add largely to their present fleet and on such terms as, I am happy to say, will not press on the pockets of the shareholders in any inconvenient way. They have arranged with a first class and highly solvent firm of

[1] v. p. 18.
[2] *Cyclopedia of New Zealand* (Christchurch, 1903), vol. III, p. 378.
[3] Some idea of life on an outward voyage by sailing ship is given in a diary of 1881, which is printed in Appendix 4.

shipbuilders to add some five ships to their fleet.' Tenders were also obtained from Alexander Stephen and Sons of Glasgow, but the quotations of Palmer's of Newcastle were apparently more advantageous. The five new ships *Orari, Otaki, Hurunui, Waipa* and *Wairoa* cost, in fact, just over £20,000 each. By the time the last of these sister ships had been delivered in 1875, the company was almost three years old and was already the owner of 13 fine sailing ships. In spite of this impressive progress, however, The N.Z.S. Co. was far from being in sole possession of the trade.

In the previous year, at the Annual General Meeting, the Chairman had said that 'the amount of business done by the company has fully realised the most sanguine expectations of the Directors, though the

Competition and Freights

9. South West India Dock, *circa* 1885. (National Maritime Museum)

rates of freight have not been equally satisfactory, owing to the competition in the shipping trade'. This competition came largely from Shaw Savill and Co. and Patrick Henderson's Albion Line. Both of these companies had been well established in the New Zealand trade

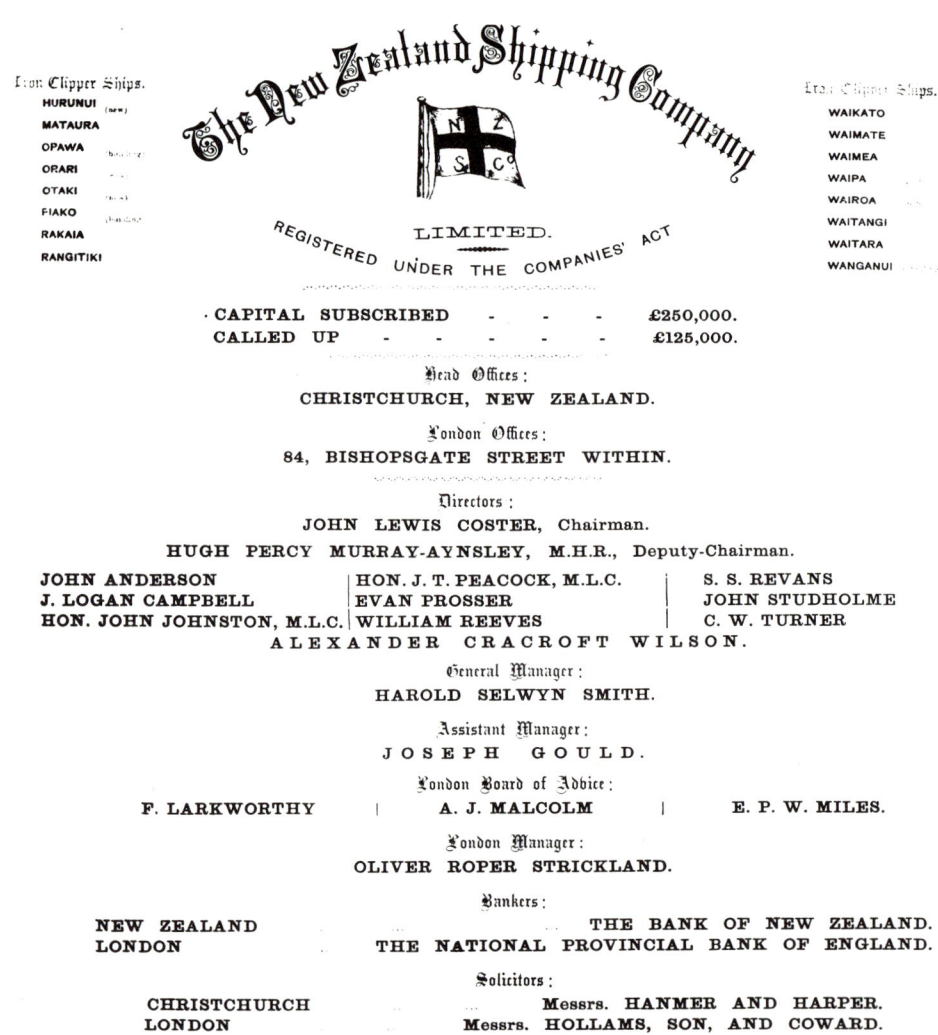

10. Title page of the company's third Annual Report, Christchurch 1876. (London Office)

for more than ten years – and were to amalgamate their interests in 1882. Interestingly enough, The N.Z.S. Co. had considered making overtures for a merger with the Albion Line as early as 1874. In this year, however, some of the advantages of an amalgamation were obtained from the fact that the three lines in the trade agreed to charge 'uniform scales of freightage, at rates which, while recognised as fair and reasonable by shippers, are remunerative to the company' (Annual Report 1875). From this time onwards, the wool rates at least seem to have been generally agreed with Shaw Savill's at the beginning of the season. It is worth illustrating the levels at which freights stood in the days of sail – the roughly equivalent rates in 1971 being shown in brackets. In a century of inflation it would be difficult to find many services which have appreciated so modestly.

In 1877 the rate for wool stood at $\frac{3}{4}$d per lb (2p). In the 1890s meat went at 1d per lb (2p), with a reduction to $\frac{3}{4}$d per lb in the off-season months of June–November. An extra $\frac{3}{4}$d per lb was charged for freezing the carcases on board the ship. Butter was reduced in 1893 from 1d to $\frac{3}{4}$d per lb (1$\frac{1}{2}$p). Outwards, rates were wonderfully simple: in 1877 it was agreed, in concert with Shaw Savill's, that the measurement rate be struck at 30s (£23.75), and rails and other weights should go at 24s (£12.75). In the same year, the passenger rate for emigrants was agreed at £14 7s 6d, with £8 7s 6d for children (£220 and £110).

In the 1880s and 1890s a sailing ship was achieving a satisfactory voyage if she could earn £3,000 gross freight on the outward leg and approximately the same on the homeward. A sailing ship often achieved only one round voyage in a year, generally outward via the Cape of Good Hope and home via Cape Horn to obtain best advantage from the prevailing winds. Today, a large refrigerated ship can, on the homeward leg alone, earn £300,000 gross freight, and may make two or three round voyages in a year. It is only fair to add that the level of disbursements has grown quite as spectacularly!

In reviewing the company's early history, it is strange to discover that what were to be the last sailing ships built specially for The N.Z.S. Co. had been delivered just four years after its foundation. The Chairman, J. L. Coster, told the Annual General Meeting of 1876, held 'in the large room of their head office, Hereford Street',

The last new building – Stephen's of Glasgow

that 'we have three new ships building – the *Piako*, *Wanganui* and *Opawa*. These I may say are being built on the Clyde this time, and gentlemen may see in the room a model of them. They are being built . . . by one of the most eminent firms on the Clyde . . . and upon such terms that the present resources of the company will be quite equal to meeting the instalments as they become due, leaving the capital of the company intact.' The London Board minutes show that tenders were received from a number of builders and that Harland and Wolff, quoting £16 2s 6d per registered ton, were bettered by Alexander Stephen at £16 os od per ton. While serving the company well for a number of years, none of the three ships was to be particularly well known for record speeds and in this respect they were to be less renowned than the ships built in the previous year by Palmer's of Newcastle.

Establishment of the cadet scheme

As well as building up the size of the fleet in these early years of the company's history, the Board was also at pains to ensure that a constant supply of good officers would be available to sail the new ships. As early as 1876 the Directors decided 'to receive on board each of their ships from three to five apprentices under indenture to the company'. What amounts to the first charter for the company's cadet scheme appears in the Chairman's report to the Annual General Meeting of 1878. He declared: 'Shareholders have always taken an interest in the appointment of apprentices. They will no doubt be interested to hear that we have now 45 apprentices on board our ships, of whom 23 are colonial youths. We have many applications now on our books. In appointing these apprentices, the Directors have been careful in the selection made. Our object has not been to get ne'er-do-wells, scapegraces that nothing can be done with, who might be sent to sea on the chances that some improvement might thereby be effected upon them. Our object is to get good steady lads, who will work their way up in our service, and become in time efficient officers and commanders of our ships.'

Early in 1879 the London Board of Advice set about 'obtaining suitable lodgings for the company's apprentices . . . in a locality convenient to the docks . . . and where necessary supervision could be supplied' (minutes of 14 March). Eventually, 92 East India Road was rented at a cost of £60 per annum, and Mrs Hodges installed as 'matron and housekeeper, at a salary of £50 per annum'. By the middle of 1880, the Board was demanding a weekly report 'of the number of apprentices in the home and their conduct'. A year later, there is a case of two particularly difficult boys and a request made for their attendance at the Board. The minute of 18 July 1881 records 'the apprentices, Manley and Cross, attended and were remonstrated with for the irregularities complained of by the matron, and desired for the future to conform more strictly to the regulations of the home'. The official record does not, unfortunately, specify the nature of the cadets' offence! Despite such occasional incidents, the institution of the cadet scheme was a far-sighted and admirable one, and it is not surprising that a Chairman of the sailing ship days could boast 'we have every good reason to be satisfied with our officers afloat'.

The year 1883 marks the climax in the history of The N.Z.S. Co.'s sailing ships. The same period saw the genesis of the two developments – steam and refrigeration – which were, in less than a generation, to render sail obsolete. Out of the total of 18 sailing ships owned by the company between 1873 and 1900, 12 were built specially for the company and six purchased from other owners. In 1883, all 18 ships were afloat and, in the words of the Annual Report, 'maintained in the highest state of efficiency'. *Pareora* and *Turakina*, the last of the sailing ships to be acquired, had recently been added to the fleet; a few weeks later *Waitara*, the first ship owned by the company, was tragically sunk in the English Channel.

Refrigeration and steam

The 1870s had seen the first successful carriage of frozen meat by sea first from South America and then from Australia to Europe. On 12 July 1881, a minute of the London Board of Advice records that the Manager tabled 'estimates of cost of refrigerating engines and a memorandum showing the probable expenditure in fitting and working one on board a sailing ship in the event of the Directors giving instructions to fit up one of the company's vessels for the conveyance of fresh meat'. Two months later, it was reported that 'a refrigerating engine had been ordered from Messrs Haslam's Engineering Co.' for installation in the *Mataura*.

In February 1882, the *Dunedin*, owned by the Albion Line, loaded at Port Chalmers 130 tons of frozen meat – the first consignment to be shipped from New Zealand to England. *Mataura* two months later followed with a further 150 tons from the same port. Subsequently, several other of the company's sailing ships were fitted with Haslam's patent refrigerating engines. Haslam was paid a royalty for all meat carried under refrigeration by the use of his machinery; this payment was reduced in 1888 from $4\frac{1}{2}$d to $2\frac{1}{4}$d per carcase. The sailing ship with the largest refrigerated capacity was *Turakina* with 39,000 cubic feet. The equipment cost some £6,000 to install, of which nearly £4,000 was spent on the engines and the remainder on the insulation. It was from these humble beginnings that The N.Z.S./ F.S.N. Companies were to develop in the next 75 years the largest fleet for the carriage of refrigerated cargoes in the world.

11. Port Chalmers, *circa* 1877. (Turnbull Library)

At the extraordinary meeting held in Christchurch in May 1882, to increase the company's capital from £250,000 to £1,000,000, it was noted that 'the refrigerated business promised to become a great accomplished fact'. But it was largely the imminent entry into steam which had precipitated the need for more capital, and the year 1883 saw the delivery of the first of the steam ships. Experimentation with the new form of propulsion had been in the air for three years. The Annual Report of August 1879 had informed shareholders that 'At the instance of the Government the full powered steamship *Stad Haarlem* was chartered by the company in conjunction with Messrs Shaw, Savill and Company of London, to bring out 600 migrants for whose passages an additional price was paid. The vessel was hired on exceptionally favourable terms, was full of passengers and cargo both out and home, and performed her voyage expeditiously and without

12. Wellington Harbour from the Terrace, *circa* 1880. (Turnbull Library)

13. Hugh Percy Murray-Aynsley, third Chairman of the New Zealand Board, 1886–1887, and again Chairman, 1893–1916. (Christchurch Boardroom)
14. Leonard Harper, fourth Chairman of the New Zealand Board, 1889–1892. (Christchurch Boardroom)

incident; the result of the charter, however, is a considerable loss, the company's moiety of which is provided for in the accounts.'

Although no one would have thought it in 1879, and in spite of the Chairman's evident lack of enthusiasm for the new means of locomotion, at that time the company had in fact already built its last two sailing ships – *Piako* and *Wanganui* – and was to purchase only two others – *Pareora* and *Turakina*. Three years later, in 1882, there was still a notable reluctance to venture with the new form of propulsion – 'the Directors, while not liking steam, were conscious that

III. *Waitangi*, oil painting reputedly by the ship's cook. (In the possession of Captain Leeman's grandson)

they should be on their guard lest the company's business should fall away whilst steam services were promoted outside'. As a result of this, on 13 June 1882, J. L. Coster, the Chairman, addressed the New Zealand Postmaster-General in the following terms: 'I have the honour to intimate that this company is now fully prepared to enter into negotiations with the Government with the view of establishing steam communication direct between the Mother country and the Colony.' The monthly service thus initiated was at first accomplished with charters, but within a year three steamers were being built, *Tongariro*, *Aorangi* and *Ruapehu* – ships which were each nearly four times the tonnage of the largest of the sailing ships, *Turakina*, and which could complete the voyage to New Zealand in under 50 days. In the years between 1883 and 1899, when the last of the sailing ships was disposed of, the company was to build 15 steamers.

The original capital of the company had been £100,000; six months after the incorporation, this was raised to £250,000. In each year from 1876 to 1884, the Directors declared a dividend of either 8% or 10% and to all outward appearance the financial fortunes of the enterprise were healthy enough. It has already been noted that the excursions into refrigeration and, more especially, into steam had given rise to a further increase in capital in 1882 to bring the total to £1,000,000. For all this, the company's finances in these years had not been husbanded as prudently as they might have been and after the publication of the annual accounts in 1884 there were serious criticisms of the way matters were being conducted. In December, a broadsheet entitled *Other People's Money* and signed 'Vanity Fair' pointedly – if a little scurrilously – enumerated the flaws in the financial position: 'We will take first the item, Fleet of Ships, Steamers, etc., – one great weakness of the company from the first has been in taking them at cost, and the reserve fund has hitherto been considered entirely as a contribution towards making up the difference in the amount they stand at in the accounts and their present actual value. But this reserve fund instead of being increased by yearly transfers, as required by Article 118, is now reduced to make up a loss of the past year, or otherwise the dividend paid has really come out of the reserve fund.... We can only exclaim with the old lady,

Finance and the transfer of control to London

15. Sir William Pearce, Bt., M.P., a Director on the London Board of Advice, 1884–1887, and on the London Board in 1888. His capital saved the company in the crisis of 1887. (Photograph by J. Russell and Sons, 1887, National Portrait Gallery)

16. Sir Edwyn Sandys Dawes, K.C.M.G., J.P., second Chairman of the London Board, 1895–1903. (From a drawing by C. W. Walton, London Office)

"it's wonderful how they do it, but they do".' The criticism, if cruel, was not unjustified, for quite inadequate sums had indeed been transferred to reserves to cover depreciation, large amounts were outstanding on secured and unsecured loans and the shareholders had a large liability in respect of uncalled capital. Further, the cost of the ships had 'been overstated chiefly by placing interest, commissions and other charges to first cost'.[1] 'Vanity Fair' also drew atten-

[1] First Report of London Board of Directors, December 1888.

17. Sir John Eldon Gorst, M.A., LL.D., F.R.S., Q.C., first Chairman of the London Board, 1888–1894. (From Sir Benjamin Stone's *Pictures*, vol. ii, London, 1906, plate 84)

18. Sir John Eldon Gorst in the House of Commons. (Drawing by F. Carruthers Gould, National Portrait Gallery)

tion to the fact that 'the shareholders are warmly congratulated upon the acquisition to the company [as a director] of one who is described by the Chairman as a very powerful man, sometimes known as "Billy the Gimlet"'. This is evidently an unflattering reference to Sir William Pearce, M.P., who as senior partner of John Elder and Company, the builders of The N.Z.S. Co's first steam ships, was one of the company's principal creditors. In spite of this expedient, it was found necessary for further calls to be made on shareholders in 1885 and 1886. The final crisis was precipitated the following year. A notice

19. City of Auckland, 1876. (Reprint published by Heritage Prints, Auckland)

to shareholders tells the story. 'The question of vesting fuller powers in the London Board of the company . . . was brought before the colonial shareholders at an extraordinary meeting . . . on 28 December 1887 at Christchurch and the views of the shareholders on the London Register were fully placed before the meeting by Mr Leonard Harper,[1] who had recently been deputed as the representative of the Directors in the colony to confer with the London Board of Advice. . . . The shareholders at that meeting determined to amend the Articles of Association, to elect several members of the Board of Advice, *viz,*

Sir C. Clifford, Bart.
Sir W. Pearce, Bart., M.P.
Sir John Gorst, Q.C., M.P.

[1] Harper was, by profession, a solicitor; he was later Chairman of the company's New Zealand Board (pp. 38–9).

Mr E. P. W. Miles
Mr T. Johnson and
Mr J. B. Westray,

Directors of the company and to transfer the principal powers formerly held by the colonial Board.' No dividend was declared during the crisis of 1886–89, but after that the corner was turned and the path of progress continued. The company which had started life as an entirely New Zealand enterprise had found it expedient to join the ranks of the great British shipping companies, although The N.Z.S. Co. Ltd. retained (as it still does) its registration as a New Zealand company.

The question of the future of the New Zealand Board after 'the transfer of the whole management of this company to London' was debated at a meeting held on 18 December 1888. Sir John Gorst, the Chairman, put the case plainly for the continuation of a colonial Board 'acting as a consultative body, carrying out the views which the London Board would from time to time intimate to them. . . . I always remember that saying of Shakespeare, if two men ride on a horse, one must ride behind; and you cannot have a double management in which each party governs with a co-ordinate authority.... You must remember it is important for us to stand well with the leading people in the colony of New Zealand. They have great influence upon freight and if they became hostile to us they could do us a great deal of harm....' Sir John's wise counsels prevailed and the company is still directed by a Board in New Zealand as well as by the main Board in London.

The Chairmen 1873–1900

The first fifteen years of the company's history is inevitably dominated by New Zealanders, most of whom had arrived from England during the 20 years before 1873.[1] The Chairmen of these early days were drawn from a cross-section of the business community of Canterbury and included a newspaper proprietor, a stock and station agent, a solicitor and a bank manager. Several of them were members of the House of Representatives, or served on the harbour board or the chamber of commerce or were members of the hunt club; all were members of their local vestry and of the Christchurch Club. Two of the original directors, who were later to serve as Chairmen, were Hugh Percy Murray-Aynsley, M.H.R. (1828–1917), a farmer and a founder of the Canterbury Frozen Meat Company, and William Reeves, M.H.R. (1825–1891), for some 30 years proprietor of *The Lyttelton Times*. Reeves was typical of the pioneers, being described by one of his staff as 'vigorous, energetic, genial, kindly, pleasant, just, business-like'. He was also a man of principle, resigning from the board of The N.Z.S. Co. in 1882 as he could not support the change from sail to steam. A later comer to the direction and eventual chairmanship was Leonard Harper, who had gone out to New Zealand with Bishop Selwyn in 1854. Another pioneer of the most adventurous sort he had, in the company of some Kaiapoi Maoris, been one of the party to make the first overland journey from Canterbury

[1] The account which follows owes much to the Macdonald *Dictionary of Canterbury Biography* in the Museum in Christchurch and the quotations given are derived from that collection. I am indebted to Mr Leonard Sharpe for much help in locating the Christchurch material for this study. A chronological list of the company's Chairmen and Directors, in New Zealand and in London, 1873–1971, is given in Appendix 1.

to the West Coast, and had returned with a sample of gold. Subsequently in the 1890s when his firm, a solicitors' business, went bankrupt Harper was indicted on eight different charges of embezzlement. He was acquitted and it was shown that there was no attempt to defraud, only a somewhat reckless over-confidence!

But to no one man does the company owe so much as to John Lewis Coster (1838–1886), its principal founder and the Chairman of the New Zealand Board for more than a decade. The son of a doctor in Exeter, Coster had emigrated to Australia at the age of 16 and started work in a bank. He was sent to New Zealand by his employers but quite soon transferred his services to the Bank of New Zealand, and later became the manager of the Christchurch branch. Although barely 30 years old, he was of sufficient standing in the city to be included in the party that went through the new tunnel on trollies a few days after it was opened – to be entertained by the contractors in Lyttelton! Besides his banking, Coster was also engaged in managing the Loan and Mercantile Agency, and this involved the chartering of ships. 'This started in his mind the idea of forming a strong New Zealand shipping company – an idea which he carried out, as no one but himself could have done it, with great firmness of will and considerable daring, in 1872' (*The Lyttelton Times*, 18 December 1886). Coster was just 34 years old. The Bank of New Zealand had recently built itself new premises in Hereford Street, and perhaps it was for this reason that The N.Z.S. Co. started life in the same locality.

Coster was, without doubt, the driving force in the company's sailing ship days, and it was appropriate, if slightly comical, that the likeness of his wife should have been carved as the figurehead of *Wanganui*, the last sailing ship built for The N.Z.S. Co.! We have a description of the still young Chairman driving into Christchurch from his home in Opawa, in a brougham drawn by a handsome pair, himself always immaculately dressed in silk hat and frock coat with a silk handkerchief protruding correctly from his pocket. Coster lived to see the advent of refrigeration and steam before his untimely death at the age of 48. Indeed, he is credited with being largely responsible for the company's building its first steamers and a complimentary banquet was held in his honour in Christchurch in August 1884, 'in recognition of the establishment of a direct steam service between Great Britain and New Zealand' (*The Canterbury Times,* 2 August). Sadly, Coster was already too ill to be present, but 'in the course of proceedings a handsome solid gold cup, valued at 200 guineas, was presented to Mr Murray-Aynsley for Mr Coster, and when this was filled with champagne and the health of Mr Coster drunk out of it by His Excellency (the Governor) and Mr Murray-Aynsley, the utmost enthusiasm was evinced by those present'. Thirteen toasts are recorded, and 'the proceedings did not close till nearly midnight'.

In spite of his astonishing achievements, it is strange that Coster, with his banking background, should have allowed the company's finances to reach the state they did by the middle 1880s.[1] Perhaps his enthusiasm outran his prudence. The obituary notice in *The Lyttelton Times* (18 December 1886) summarises the qualities of this remarkable man – 'In business keen, bold, daring, smart, progressive and energetic; in his private life a pleasant, cheery companion, a kind hospitable host and open-handed and generous to a fault.'

The period 1888–1904, during which the first two Chairmen, Sir John Eldon Gorst and Sir Edwyn Sandys Dawes, presided over the London Board, covers the consolidation of the financial fortunes of the company and the revolution which was accomplished when steam finally beat sail. The personalities of these two men merit some description.

After a distinguished career at Cambridge, where he was third wrangler, John Eldon Gorst (1835–1916) went out to New Zealand in 1860. Making a name for himself with Sir George Grey, the Governor, and espousing the cause of the Maori, he was made Civil Commissioner in the Upper Waikato and acted as an intermediary between the Government and the Kingites during the Maori Wars of the 1860s. He published a book in 1864, *The Maori King,* and another towards the end of his life, in 1908, *New Zealand Revisited, Recollections of the Days of my Youth.* Returning to England, Gorst was called to the Bar in 1865, entered Parliament as Member for Cambridge and was later Member for Chatham. A staunch supporter of Disraeli, he later joined Sir Henry Drummond-Wolff, Lord Randolph Churchill and A. J. Balfour to form the 'Fourth Party' – a ginger group within the Conservative Opposition. When the

[1] v. pp. 33–7.

MR. ISAAC GIBBS.
CHRISTCHURCH.

J B Westray

20. James Brown Westray, a Director on the London Board of Advice, 1887, and on the London Board, 1888–1905. J. B. Westray & Co. Ltd. became passenger, cargo and insurance brokers for The N.Z.S. Co. in the early 1890s. (Photograph reproduced in *Westrays* by Alan Fagg, London, 1957)

21. Isaac Gibbs, Secretary of the company in New Zealand, 1880–1892, and General Manager, 1892–1914. Caricature published by *The Press*, Christchurch, 1901. (Christchurch Boardroom)

Tories, under Lord Salisbury, ousted Gladstone in 1885, Gorst became Solicitor-General in the new Government. Back in Opposition again by 1888, Sir John Gorst was prevailed upon to become the first Chairman of the London Board of The New Zealand Shipping Company. Politics continued to occupy much of his time and occasionally, in the Board minutes, they positively intruded! The meeting of 9 August 1888 has the comment: 'At this stage of the proceedings, the Chairman (it being India Budget day) was compelled to leave for the House of Commons.' Gorst's connection with the company ended

22. 'Hymeneal Feast . . . Immolation of Isaac'. This cartoon, by W. A.
Bowring, was issued in 1901 in *The Weekly Press*, a paper published by the
Christchurch Press Co. Ltd. It caricatures Isaac Gibbs, together with some of
his fellow members of the Canterbury Club:

J. Bickerton Fisher (with skewer and tartan socks), Solicitor, of Garrick,
   Cowlishaw & Fisher.
Isaac Gibbs (in pot, with The N.Z.S. Co. flag), third General Manager of the
   company.
J. J. Kinsey (with chopper and Tyser Line flag – which was later adopted by
   the Port Line), partner Kinsey Barns & Co., agents for Tyser Line Ltd.
F. M. Wallace (with violin), leading musician of the town.
A. Carrick (with concertina), President Christchurch Golf Club.
E. G. Staveley (with carrots), Manager N.Z. Loan & Mercantile Agency Co. of
   N.Z. Ltd.
James Embling (horse and rider), Manager Bank of New Zealand.
W. C. Hill (on barrel), Director Manning's Brewery.
John Anderson (with glengarry and bottle), Managing Director of Anderson's
   Ltd. and a Director of The N.Z.S. Co.
J. H. Hall (with turkey), sheepfarmer of Motunau – previously leading grocer
   of Christchurch. His brother was accountant of The N.Z.S. Co.
A. W. Bennett (carrying front end of case), Lyttelton manager of The N.Z.S. Co.
   and assistant to Isaac Gibbs. Later, on Gibbs's death, he succeeded as
   General Manager.
Fred H. Barns (with Huddart Parker flag), Partner Kinsey Barns & Co. In his
   earlier days he was an officer and a Captain in The N.Z.S. Co.'s fleet. After
   his death the firm was changed to Kinsey & Co. Ltd.

(Christchurch Boardroom)

in 1894 and it was announced that 'The Right Hon. Sir John Gorst,
having accepted office under the Government, has resigned his seat
on the Board.' One of the last glimpses we have of Gorst is in 1902
when, as the guest of Sir Ernest and Lady Cassel, he cruised up the

Nile on a *dahabeeyah* with, among others, the son of his old friend Lord Randolph, the young Winston Churchill.

At the age of 16, Edwyn Sandys Dawes (1838–1904)[1] had his first introduction to the sea and ships, becoming a sailor and seeing service throughout the Crimean War. He reached the rank of Chief Officer with the P & O and travelled widely in India and China up to 1865. During this period he narrowly escaped death off the coast of Sumatra, when he was shipwrecked and spent five days in an open boat before being picked up and taken to Singapore. After working for a time in the offices of Mackinnon, Mackenzie in Calcutta, Dawes returned to England and with John Gray founded Gray, Dawes and Co. Now Duncan Mackinnon was a great friend of J. B. Westray, who had been on the London Board of Advice since 1887, and it was through this connection that E. S. Dawes came into contact with The N.Z.S. Co. The already parlous financial condition of the company coupled with the death in 1888 of Sir William Pearce, M.P., who had upwards of a quarter of a million pounds invested in the company, meant that both considerable capital and considerable ability were required to rescue the whole enterprise. Edwyn Sandys Dawes provided both.[2] During the decade of his Chairmanship the sailing ships were gradually phased out and no less than 13 steamships were built.

His interests were very diverse and included directorships of companies trading with Africa and India, as well as Australia and New Zealand. He was a Member of the Council of Administration of the Suez Canal, and was for a time Chairman of the Committee of Management of HMS *Worcester*. In the same year as he became Chairman of The N.Z.S. Co., he was created K.C.M.G. in recognition of the part he played in the development of relations between Britain and her Colonies.

As has been already described, the entire fleet of 18 sailing ships was acquired – by purchase or building – in just ten years, between 1873

The last days of sail

[1] This account of Sir Edwyn Dawes owes much to *Westrays, a Record of J. B. Westray & Co. Ltd.* by Alan Fagg (London, 1957).

[2] The transfer of the Pearce interest was not accomplished without opposition. This is recorded in self-righteous, if disgruntled, fashion by Thomas Johnson, a Director, in a printed *Narrative of Events* addressed to the shareholders. It runs to 38 pages and is dated 28 November 1889.

23. Panorama of Lyttelton Harbour, *circa* 1880. The fourth and seventh ships from the right are *City of Perth* (later *Turakina*) and *Mataura* respectively. (Turnbull Library)

and 1883. By 1893, nearly ten steamers had been built, and the number of sailing ships had fallen to the same number. In 1895, the Chairman, Sir Edwyn Dawes, outlined the policy with regard to the sailing ships – 'These ships were built about 20 years ago for an entirely different condition of things to that which now prevails. At that time the whole of the direct passenger trade with New Zealand was carried on by sailing ships and our ships were all built with large poops for the accommodation of passengers and are rather poor cargo carriers. At the present time, as doubtless you know, all passengers go by steamers, consequently our sailing ships are carrying about huge passenger encumbrances to no purpose and, in competition with more modern sailing vessels and cargo steamers, it is impossible

for them to hold their own; we shall therefore take every opportunity that offers of getting rid of them.'

That rather prosaic chronicle, the company's Annual Report, dismissed – without any apparent display of sentiment – the last of the sailing ships on 11 October 1899: 'It will be noted that sailing ships no longer appear in the Assets of the company, the last four having been disposed of at prices slightly in excess of the book value.' It is, however, perhaps more gracious to take leave of the days of sail, and of those who served the sailing ships of The N.Z.S. Co., with the Chairman's words, delivered in Christchurch in 1880:

'We have a very efficient, good and zealous staff in London, where we are very well represented. In the Colony, too, our officers are zealous and efficient doing the work well in every part, and afloat, our captains and ships' officers, and also our apprentice boys and our men, will honourably compare with any other body of men afloat.'

24. *Waitara* off Gravesend, 6 July 1879. She was the first ship owned by The N.Z.S. Co. (National Maritime Museum)

The Sailing Ships

Hindostan was an iron ship, built for the British and Eastern Shipping Co. Ltd. in 1863 by J. Reid and Co. of Glasgow. She was a ship of 883 gross tons and her dimensions were approximately 182 feet by 31 feet by 21 feet. The *Hindostan* and the *Dunfillan*, which were both purchased by The N.Z.S. Co. towards the end of 1873, were described at a special general meeting of the company as 'fine iron ships built under survey with extra strength'. On her first voyage under new management, *Hindostan* sailed from London on 12 September 1873 and arrived in Auckland 108 days later on 28 December – a long voyage even for the days of sail. She only once exceeded this, in 1879, when her outward voyage took 109 days. In 1875 *Waitara* – her name was changed in 1874 – was properly fitted out for the conveyance of emigrants. Her length was apparently increased by 9 feet to 191 feet in 1881.

Waitara completed less than ten voyages for the company, for she met with sudden disaster in 1883 in the English Channel, when she collided with another of the company's vessels, *Hurunui*. The tragedy was very fully reported in *The Times* during June and July of that year. Both ships, leaving London together, 'landed their pilots, discharged their tugs and beat down the Channel against a south westerly wind. About 10 p.m. (26 June) they were 25 miles off the Bill of Portland, both close hauled. . . . It had just ceased raining but the moon was quite hidden in the mist.' *Hurunui* was on starboard tack and *Waitara* on the port – it was therefore the duty of the latter to keep out of the way. This she failed to do and *Hurunui* 'struck the ill-starred vessel just about the saloon on the starboard side . . . rebounded and struck again'. According to one of the passengers, 'two minutes would almost have covered the time from the moment when the *Waitara* was struck till she was beneath the waves'. She had a crew of 28, besides eight passengers aboard. Of these only 16 were saved; the second officer, whose mistake had caused the disaster, went down with the ship. 'Captain Webster of *Waitara* had a miraculous

Waitara (ex Hindostan)

escape [being] caught in the rigging [of *Hurunui*] and absolutely dragged away from his ship, but he instantly returned to it in a life-boat'. The 'damage to *Hurunui* was confined to the watertight bulk-head'. Her Captain was 'indefatigable in his exertions' to assist the survivors and it was 'impossible to speak too highly of the officers and men'. In the enquiry, the master of the *Waitara* was blamed for not carrying his boats in their davits in the Channel and, in the judg-ment of the Wreck Commissioner's Court, 'the blame rested entirely between the master and second officer of the *Waitara*'.

This disaster, coupled with the sinking in the Channel about the same time of an emigrant ship bound for Tasmania, resulted in the embarkation of passengers at Plymouth rather than London for many years. These circumstances explain why many of the company's

25. *Mataura* in dry dock at Port Chalmers. (Turnbull Library)

IV. *Waimate*, water colour by J. Spurling, 1927. (London Office). This picture was printed in *Sail, the romance of the clipper ships*, by J. Spurling and Basil Lubbock, London, 1929, vol. ii, facing p. 72

steamships (including *Rangitiki* and *Rangitata*) were registered in Plymouth. This tradition lasted until 1947 when *Haparangi* became the first of the company's new ships in modern times to be registered in London.

Before her acquisition by the company, *Dunfillan* had already made one voyage to New Zealand – in 1870 when she was still in the hands of her original owner, W. Ross. She had been built in 1868 by Aitken and Mansell of Glasgow and was an iron ship of 898 gross tons. Her dimensions were approximately 199 feet by 33 feet by 20 feet. Like *Waitara*, she was acquired towards the end of 1873, but did not actually arrive at Dunedin until 15 January 1874, after a voyage of 80 days.

Mataura (ex Dunfillan)

Mataura – her name was changed in 1874 – completed 13 voyages to New Zealand of which only one, her last, in 1894 took more than 100 days. Her voyage to Nelson in 1875 was, according to the Immigration Commissioner's report, 'a severe one owing to extensive fields of ice encountered by the ship in a low latitude'. Considerable discomfort was experienced from chilblains and frost-bite, and there were actually 14 deaths reported. The report of the ship's Surgeon-Superintendent in November 1877 sheds some amusing sidelights on the pastimes of those on board. It complains that letters had been passed 'behind the stringers of the ship's side between the single and married quarters' and also from members of the crew to girls on board. The report tersely recommends that the spaces that make this correspondence possible should be closed! The passengers during this voyage certainly appear to have enjoyed themselves for, in a letter to Captain A. Brown, subscribed to by 184 passengers, they express themselves thus: 'We the Emigrants on board the ship *Mataura* for Hawke's Bay in taking leave of you beg to tender our grateful and heartfelt thanks for the many acts of kindness received at your hands. Our passage by your excellent management has been a great pleasure, the remembrance of which, together with your genial goodness and manly exertion on our behalf, was a source of delight.' *Mataura*'s best voyage was in 1880, when she made the passage from London to Dunedin in 76 days. As *The Otago Daily Times* noted, she was 'in splendid order . . . a notable pace-maker; the good

26. *Mataura* in dry dock at Port Chalmers. (Turnbull Library)

ship fully justifies the encomiums which we have already passed upon her'.

An experiment was made with *Mataura* in 1882 which had momentous results for the future history of the company. At a cost of £5,000 Haslam's patent dry-air refrigerator had been installed.[1] The voyage during which it was first put to the test was later described by her master, Captain H. E. Greenstreet, from extracts from the ship's log: 'The barque was being insulated at the fore end. Mr (now Sir) Alfred Haslam was accidentally shut up in a small refrigerated chamber, and would have frozen to death had he not been discovered in time. . . . Left London 15th December [1881] . . . fish and birds shot in Southern Ocean, were put in the chamber, and on arrival at Lyttelton were presented to Sir Julius Von Haast for the Christchurch Museum. . . . 27th April, made fast to Port Chalmers wharf,

[1] An account of this machine and its use aboard *Mataura* in 1882 is printed in Appendix 3.

27. *Mataura* at Port Chalmers. This photograph would appear to date from 1874–75, i.e. after the ship's name had been changed to *Mataura* but before she had been painted in the company's colours adopted in 1875. (v. p. 22) (Turnbull Library)

150 carcases per day were sent on board and frozen in 'tween decks for 24 hours, then bagged and stowed in lower hold. The meat cargo consisted of 3,844 carcases of mutton, 24 quarters beef and 77 pigs: total weight, 322,092 lbs, freight £3,340. The voyage home lasted 103 days, and great worry was experienced as the boiler pumps would not act on one tack when the ship heeled over. The voyage was a success, and the meat was delivered in excellent condition.'[1] The Chairman reported at the Annual General Meeting in August, however, that the freight of $2\frac{1}{2}$d per lb had 'not proved a financial success to the company'. He further commented that the Albion Company had lost heavily by their ship *Dunedin*, which had sailed in February from Port Chalmers carrying the first refrigerated cargo from New Zealand. *Mataura*, which sailed in June, was the second refrigerated

[1] J. T. Critchell and J. Raymond, *A History of the Frozen Meat Trade* (London, 1912), p. 370.

28. Captain Herbert E. Greenstreet, Master of *Mataura* when she carried her first refrigerated cargo, 1882. (From *A History of the Frozen Meat Trade*, p. 370)

ship from that port. However, it is perhaps of interest that, whereas in the case of *Dunedin* the New Zealand and Australian Land Company chartered the refrigerated space of the ship for meat at a freight of $2\frac{1}{4}$d per lb and the cargo was insured at a premium of five guineas per cent, neither safeguard was possible with *Mataura*, and the venture was the shipowner's risk. She returned next year and lifted the first refrigerated cargo ever to be shipped from Auckland. On the homeward passage, on this occasion, a game of snow-balling was played at the Equator! It may be noted that ten years later Captain Greenstreet was in command of the ss *Ruahine* which had a refrigerated carrying capacity of about 30 times that of *Mataura*. Captain Greenstreet lived to be a veteran master, making 80 round voyages and sailing, or steaming, two million miles.

Mataura was eventually sold by the company in 1895 to Captain Bruusguard of Drammen in Norway for £2,800 and renamed *Alida*.

Her end came in August 1900 when she was dismasted and abandoned in the Pacific Ocean. However, it is perhaps better to conclude her story with the words of *The Lyttelton Times* of January 1887, describing *Mataura*'s arrival in New Zealand: 'She came into port, as is usual with the vessels of this company, in excellent order, both on deck and aloft.'

Rangitiki was in many ways the pride of the sailing ships, being one of the largest ever owned by the company, a record pace-maker, and completing an astonishing career of some 60 years' service. *Scimitar* had been built in 1863 by Martin Samuelson of Hull for Finlay Campbell and Co.; by 1872 she had been transferred to J. K. Welch, from whom she was purchased by The N.Z.S. Co. in 1873. Her name was changed to *Rangitiki* by the middle of 1874. Her dimensions were approximately 210 feet by 35 feet by 23 feet. She was an iron ship of 1,227 gross tons. Her rig was changed from that of a clipper ship to a barque after 1889.

Rangitiki (ex Scimitar)

Scimitar retained her name for her first voyage under the company's flag. *The Otago Daily Times* described her arrival on 6 March 1874: 'We have to report that the *Scimitar* is a remarkably handsome vessel, being purchased in December 1873 . . . subsequently put into dry-dock and received a thorough overhaul – nearly a re-rig from deck to truck. Most of her spars are new. That she is a clipper is evident by the remarkable passage she has made from Plymouth, the quickest on record – the time being 67 days from land to land.' In fact, the passage from Plymouth to Port Chalmers, port to port, had taken 71 days, a record which stood for more than 25 years, until 1900. Her land to land time for this voyage was, however, bettered by one day in 1888 by Shaw Savill's *Westland*. Altogether, *Rangitiki* was an extraordinarily and consistently fast clipper; in 1876 she completed a round voyage to New Zealand in just under seven months. On the same voyage, she covered 345 miles in one day – an average of $14\frac{1}{2}$ knots – a speed not far short of her later motor-ship namesake!

The voyage of 1873–74 was notable, however, for reasons other than speed. The combined effect of scarlet fever, bronchitis, measles, diarrhoea and variola accounted for no less than 26 deaths. However, in spite of these calamities, there was a brighter side. *The Otago Daily Times* continues: 'Hymen's torch was also kindled on a memorable Sabbath when a strapping young Norwegian named Michael Olson was spliced by Captain Fox in a sailor-like manner to Matthia Christenson also of Norwegian birth ... much pleasant hilarity was occasioned by the circumstance.' There were also four births on the voyage; Dr Hoskings, with some reason therefore, remarked: 'What between reading divine service every Sunday, the marriage, the baptisms and burying so many, there was enough work on the passage to have kept a parson employed.' Generally, the press report concludes: 'Both the Doctor and Captain spoke in high terms of the emigrants that were on board. . . . The appearance of the emigrants was also in their favour. The women looked healthy and comely, a few of the men were stalwart, whilst the majority seemed wanting in phisique (*sic*), at least of those who lined the ship's bulwark [on arrival] the majority were undersized and wore the expression of life in large towns.'

29. *Rangitiki* being towed to Dunedin. The funnel amidships belongs to the second tug. (Turnbull Library)

30. *Rangitiki* under sail, from a painting by Stanley Pellett. (Photograph, London Office)

The incidents which were experienced on two voyages of the *Rangitiki* are gruesome reminders of the hazards of navigation in the days of the sailing ships.[1] During the outward passage of 1883, according to a passenger 'we sighted what we took to be a raft with five human beings on it, all awash. The lifeboat was lowered, and we rescued two men who had been on a deck house (not a raft) for two days and nights. Eight men scrambled on this house when they left the wreck of the *Kenmore Castle*, but six were washed off.' Later, seven men were rescued from another wreck, the barquentine *Maria Agathe*: 'It was very risky work owing to the heavy seas.... We had to get close enough to the wreck's lee quarter to allow one man at a time to jump in and then back away as the lifeboat at one time would be almost level with the ship's rail, and three seconds later 20 feet below.' The last rescue on this voyage occurred when a doctor aboard *Rangitiki* was called to tend 'a young fellow [aboard the *James Grimsby*] who had been suffering with a broken arm for 28 days. The arm was amputated and the man greatly relieved.'

The tragedies of the other voyage (in 1897) were presaged in melo-

[1] *White Wings*, pp. 255–7.

31. *Rangitiki* under sail, from a painting. (Turnbull Library)

dramatic fashion – a cat which had jumped aboard the *Rangitiki* from a wool-lighter in Napier had next day leapt to its death from a porthole. The following morning a great wind arose from the east, and in spite of the fact that all the cable was out the ship started dragging towards the shore. Captain Pottinger was just considering how the heavy strain could be eased on the windlass when a huge sea crashed on board, carrying away the after end of the deck house and hurling him into the sea. His body was recovered, but his neck was found to be broken, death having apparently been instantaneous.

With the advent of steam, *Rangitiki* was one of the last of the sailing ships to be disposed of by the company, passing to the control of Skibsacties Dalston, Norwegian owners, in 1899 and renamed by them *Dalston*. She disappeared from Lloyd's in 1911, but was subsequently sold to a French owner and named *Paul Bouket*, taken to Noumea and used as a hulk. She was reported as being in use in Australian waters between 1914–18 and, after the war, returned to Noumea.

Rangitiki had a unique career – only half of it in fact with The N.Z.S. Co. Her record as a great and gracious clipper is neatly summed up by *The Lyttelton Times* on her arrival after an extremely fast land to land passage of 67 days in 1876: 'The appearance of the vessel was everything that could be wished for.'

Waimea was the smallest sailing ship ever owned by the company, being purchased in 1874; her dimensions were approximately 194 feet by 32 feet by 19 feet and she was of 871 gross tons. She was an iron ship having been built by Godeffroy of Hamburg in 1868 and

Waimea (ex Dorette)

32. Model of *Rangitiki*: overall length 16″. (London Office)

then named *Dorette*. Although *Waimea* – her name was changed in 1874 – remained under the company's flag for more than 20 years, she seems to have enjoyed a fairly uneventful career. She made over 20 voyages to New Zealand, but less than half took under 100 days. Her fastest voyage was in 1874 when she reached Auckland from England in 76 days, land to land. *The New Zealand Herald* of 15 April, reporting her arrival, said there were 319 emigrants, 43 head of cattle, 1 horse and 250 sheep aboard – an amazing collection for such a small ship!

In June 1875, an agreement was reached in London with Sir Julius Vogel of the New Zealand Government and the Agent-General, whereby the company undertook 'the whole of the Government emigration and cargo business', after an unsuccessful attempt to

33. *Waimea* at Port Chalmers. (Turnbull Library)

agree terms with Shaw Savill and Co., Ltd. for a part of the contract. The rate for adults was to be £16 and for children £9 per head. The increase from the original rate of £14 10s for adults had been brought about as a result of 'the cost of extra dietary and medical comforts', as the Board minutes rather grandly proclaim. *Waimea* was one of the first ships to sail under the new conditions. The result was evidently a reasonable success for, despite four deaths on the outward voyage, a letter from the Immigration Commissioner of October 1876, reporting on his inspection of the ship, declared: 'The usual questions were asked as to any complaints, and were replied to by three cheers for the Captain and Doctor.' In more tangible terms, it was customary in such circumstances for a gratuity of £25 to be paid to the master and 10s 'per soul landed alive' to the Surgeon-Superintendent!

34. *Waimea* off Gravesend, 17 July 1875. (National Maritime Museum)

One of the more exciting incidents in the ship's career occurred in June 1893, when she was sailing from Wellington to Boston: 'After rounding the Horn a terrific explosion occurred one day, and so much damage was done that she had to put into Rio for repairs. The origin of the explosion was never traced, but it was thought that it was caused by a boy named Clements, who was blown to pieces. This was the only casualty. Everyone on board got a great scare, and felt that the ship had had a most providential escape.'[1]

Waimea was sold in 1895 for £2,450 to Westergaard and Co. of Norway. She retained her name, although her colours were changed—a photograph exists of the ship at Port Chalmers under her new ownership. However, she survived only a short time, being wrecked in September 1902 on the South African coast, after 35 years' service.

[1] *White Wings*, p. 296.

35. *Rakaia* at Dunedin. (Turnbull Library)

36. Captain John Bone in 1880; he was Master of the *Rakaia* 1881–1882 and later Marine Superintendent in New Zealand. He retired in 1924 after 50 years' service with The N.Z.S. Co. (From *White Wings*, p. 289)

This ship, besides being the first vessel to be built for the company, *Rakaia* was the first of four sister ships built by J. Blumer and Co. of Sunderland. She was registered with Lloyd's in November 1873 and was an iron ship of 1,057 gross tons. Her dimensions were approximately 210 feet by 34 feet by 19 feet. She completed nearly 20 voyages to New Zealand for the company, but only on two occasions bettered 90 days on her outward passage. *The Lyttelton Times* of 27 April 1874, reporting on the ship on her arrival on her maiden voyage when she took out 333 passengers, commented on her appearance and particularly her speed: 'Looking at the ship from a distance she has a splendid spring from fore to aft, but the mainmast is placed somewhat too far aft which reduces her speed.' The account goes on to say that the saloon was elegantly furnished, the cabins commodious and capable of holding three persons; they were exceedingly well finished, the timber being of teak and birdseye maple with gilt mouldings, and fitted with every requisite. Below, 'the galleys are certainly the best that we have seen on any vessel, everything of the greatest neatness and the places being well ventilated'. Besides due consideration being given to the hygienic qualities of the accommodation, care was also apparently given to the personal condition of the passengers during the voyage. Objections to this interference are evinced by a petition, signed by 98 passengers, on 20 September 1878, against the compulsory sale of yellow soap at one shilling per bar, before *Rakaia* set sail from Plymouth!

Rakaia achieved her best land to land voyage, of 78 days, when Captain John Bone took her out to Auckland in 1881. According to *The New Zealand Herald* of the time she brought out 'a large number of passengers, a considerable proportion of whom come with well-lined pockets'. Some of her cargo is also mentioned with a note of some of its values: clothing and textiles £10,000; straw hats £430; 1,240 gallons of brandy; 2,210 gallons of British spirit; six tons of candles. The total value came to £30,000.

Captain Bone was one of the most notable of the company's early masters, making no less than 52 voyages to New Zealand in sail and steam (at that time a record), and finally retiring in 1924 from the position of the company's first Marine Superintendent in New Zealand, after 50 years' service with the company. Admiral Lord Jellicoe as Governor-General attended the farewell luncheon given in his honour aboard *Remuera*. The Prime Minister, W. F. Massey, in proposing the toast of the guest of honour, said he had travelled to New Zealand 54 years previously aboard a ship in which Captain Bone was serving as an apprentice. He had known him ever since and came to regard him as one of his most intimate friends.

The extent to which a speedy passage in the days of sail was due to the experience of the navigator is suggested by an incident on the outward voyage to Wellington in 1880 when Mr Hamon, the second mate,[1] was making his first voyage to New Zealand. Coming through the Cook Strait, approaching Wellington Heads with extra caution, he kept too far to sea; a north-westerly gale sprang up and although

[1] Later the commander of *Turakina* when she accomplished her celebrated feat of overhauling the steamer *Ruapehu*, v. p. 106.

the lighthouse could be seen, the *Rakaia* did not enter the Heads till three weeks later!

Rakaia was sold in 1892 at a time when several of the sailing ships were being disposed of; she was bought by J. N. Rodbertus, of Barth, Germany, and renamed *Marie*. In 1906 she was sunk but refloated, and passing five years later to the ownership of Revere Co. and registered in Barbados she was again named *Rakaia*. By 1916 her owners had altered her name to *Ruth Stark* and changing hands yet again in 1918 she became *Monte Carlo* under the French flag. By 1919 she finally disappeared from Lloyd's, after a recorded career of nearly 50 years.

Waikato

Registered with Lloyd's in January 1874, this ship was the sister of *Rakaia* in all her specifications except her gross tonnage, which is given as 1,053 tons. She completed 12 voyages to New Zealand under the company's flag and, while never setting any records for speed,

37. *Waikato* in Port Chalmers dry dock. (Turnbull Library)

she only exceeded 100 days on the outward passage on three occasions. Two of her most notable performances were in 1877 when she made the voyage from Plymouth to Lyttelton, land to land, in 78 days, and in 1876 when she reached Plymouth Docks from Wellington in the very short time of 76 days.

On her maiden voyage she was well reported upon by the Commissioner of Immigration. He declared: 'We believe the *Waikato* is one of the best immigrant ships which has come into this port [Wellington]. She was remarkably clean and the people were all in good health.' The following year the schoolmaster on board had difficulties which almost halted his labours; he pitifully reported: 'I found that I never could recover at the end of each evening the number of books and slates which I had given out at the commencement so that the school materials continued to diminish. I was forced to discontinue these classes until such time as all the missing books, etc., should be returned.'

38. *Waikato* forcing a passage through a barrier of pack ice, 26 July 1878. (From *The Graphic*, London, October 1878)

Probably one of *Waikato*'s most memorable voyages was her homeward run from Lyttelton in 1878. *The Graphic* printed an eye-witness account in October: 'On the 25th July last in lat. 57° S., long. 58° W., after passing several large icebergs (one about two miles long and several hundred feet high), the *Waikato* was completely surrounded by pack ice. . . . As night was coming on, and the only clear passage visible was right to windward, Captain Worster resolved, if possible, to keep his vessel in the space between the two barriers until daylight. This was no easy undertaking, as the night was 16 hours long, and there were, every now and then, very heavy snow squalls. During these squalls the vessel struck against a great many pieces of ice, and twice went through a barrier, but fortunately kept free of the bergs.' Captain Worster then takes up the story: 'I did not like the idea of remaining in the ice another night, especially as the weather began to look threatening. I therefore steered for the pack and, picking out a place where the pieces appeared smallest, got through not without a good many hard knocks. After getting through we had comparatively clear water and, on the following day,

not a particle of ice was to be seen. Had we, while in the ice, encountered boisterous weather and rough seas, I am fully persuaded
we should never have got through, the *Waikato* being an iron ship,
and therefore not able to stand the knocks and rubs we should have
received.'

The company sold *Waikato* in 1888 to German owners and she
was renamed *J. C. Pflueger*. After being picked up in a dismasted
condition, she passed to the ownership of J. D. Spreckels and Co. in
1901, was converted into a four-masted barquentine and named
Coronado. Passing through the ownership of several American companies she disappeared from Lloyd's after being reported as having
'foundered' in November 1913 while in the ownership of the Canadian Pacific Railway Company.[1]

[1] According to *White Wings*, p. 295, 'She was later sold to the Canadian Pacific
Coal Co. She foundered on 20 November 1918 when being towed from Ladysmith
to Vancouver'.

39. *Waitangi* at Port Chalmers. (Turnbull Library)

Waitangi

Built by J. Blumer and Co. of Sunderland, she was an iron ship of 1,161 gross tons and was registered with Lloyd's in June 1874. Her dimensions were 222 feet by 35 feet by 21 feet. Although very similar, of course, in specifications to her sister ship *Waimate*, she did not enjoy her notable record for consistently fast passages. *Waitangi* made some 25 voyages to New Zealand and on no less than ten occasions exceeded 100 days on the outward voyage. Her best outward run was to Lyttelton in 1883–84 when she completed the passage in 77 days. On this occasion she was carrying 312 passengers, of whom the majority consisted of immigrants.

Like *Waimate*, *Waitangi* was excellently provided with boats in case of emergency. One authority says she had 'six splendid large boats, two lifeboats properly fitted up; two large pinnace boats, ready to launch at a moment's notice, one large cutter and a large gig'. On one voyage – to Auckland in 1895 – very severe gales were met with and the lifeboats were smashed, rails carried away, everything on deck washed overboard and the saloon and cabins flooded. Several sails were also blown away; the total passage had taken 117 days.

40. *Waitangi* under sail, from a painting. (Turnbull Library)

But it is *Waitangi*'s near loss by fire on more than one occasion which perhaps provides the most memorable part of her story. An amusing letter exists, dated 11 October 1877, written by a Mr H. Selwyn-Smith, and also signed by Captain Hodder and the Surgeon-Superintendent; it is addressed to the Immigration Officer in New Zealand. It complains that 'the immigrants positively refused to go through the drudgery of fire drill. It was deemed advisable as the Captain had no power to enforce the orders...not to persist in a course which would only have led to a disturbance.... However, great confidence [was placed] on his crew who were well disciplined and thoroughly acquainted with their duties in respect of the occurrence of fire.'

On another occasion, however, the precaution of fire drill proved of real value. Mr William Mackenzie, a passenger, in describing the incident, says: 'There was considerable excitement when the alarm was given. Fortunately, when the real thing came the sailors and single men, all well drilled, promptly took up their respective positions. The duty of the single men was to get their blankets up, place them in water and then throw them over the fire, as was done on this occasion. The blankets were destroyed, and the men had no others during the passage. Fortunately the fire was soon got under, without any serious loss being sustained.'

The voyage to Lyttelton in 1875 nearly finished in disaster on account of the hazard of fire. *The Lyttelton Times* of the day described the incident in which one of the stewards and the assistant baker were discovered in the storeroom helping themselves to some of the contents. To assist them in their theft a candle had been 'placed on top of the powder magazine...one shudders to think of the catastrophe that might have taken place'. As a correspondent disgustedly commented, the deed was committed 'to satisfy a miserable lust for liquor!' The arrival of the ship otherwise drew from the newspaper qualified approval. Her passengers are described as 'appearing to be a thoroughly respectable and intelligent body of people', and *Waitangi* is proclaimed 'the favourite ship of The New Zealand Shipping Company's fleet'.

Passing to Norwegian ownership in 1899, *Waitangi* was renamed *Agda*. Her end came in January 1913 when Lloyd's reported her as having foundered.

41. Captain Thomas Leeman, Master of *Waitangi*, 1884–1890. (In the possession of Captain Leeman's grandson)

42. Barometer from the *Waitangi*: overall size 7 ins. (In the possession of Captain Leeman's grandson)

The sister ship of *Rakaia*, *Waikato* and *Waitangi*, *Waimate*[1] was the last of four ships to be built by J. Blumer and Co. of Sunderland for the company. She was registered with Lloyd's in August 1874. She was of 1,157 gross tons and her dimensions were 220 feet by 35 feet by 21 feet.

The report on her maiden voyage survives among the National Archives in Wellington. The Surgeon-Superintendent, George Cleghorn, was generally enthusiastic but noted 'the way in which the food (especially pea soup, porridge and rice) was cooked was far from satisfactory, owing to its getting burnt, through the large size

[1] The diary of a passenger on an outward voyage of *Waimate* is printed in Appendix 4.

of the boiler, which prevented the cook from getting at it to stir it'.

Unlike *Waitangi*, *Waimate* had a good record for fast voyages and out of her 22 outward passages she broke 90 days no less than nine times. Her finest achievement, however, was in 1880–81 when she accomplished the voyage from London to Lyttelton in 74 days. This was a record which, it is said, remained unbeaten until 1900. *The Lyttelton Times* of 8 January 1881 described her appearance on arrival: 'The *Waimate* was in splendid order, the passengers' quarters in the 'tween decks being scrupulously clean, while everything about her decks and aloft was as clean and neat as work could make it. The passengers all seemed highly pleased with Captain Peek and at the end of the passage presented him with a purse of sovereigns and an address in which they referred most feelingly to his skill, intrepidity and self-possession during the very perilous time in the Channel,

43. *Waimate* off Gravesend, 27 October 1874. (National Maritime Museum)

44. *Waimate* at Port Chalmers. (Turnbull Library)

and the unvarying kindness and urbanity shown to all.'

On the homeward run immediately subsequent to her outward record, *Waimate* narrowly escaped disaster. One of the crew who was on board at the time described the story: 'The *Waimate* after leaving Lyttelton on the run to Cape Horn, possibly owing to the lack of suitable opportunities for obtaining observations, suddenly found herself land-locked off the Patagonian coast. The position was critical, inasmuch as the *Waimate*, like all vessels making the three months' trip home, had unshackled the cables from her anchors and run them down into the chain locker in the fore part of the ship. The anchors had been hoisted inboard by the aid of special tackle rigged for that purpose, and were lashed very securely on the fo'c'sle head as it was not anticipated they would be required for many weeks. It was in this condition that the *Waimate* found herself on a dark and dirty night off a rocky, rugged coast, full of indentations, with very deep water right up to cliffs – very much the same as the West Coast Sounds in New Zealand. There was no anchorage. It would have been folly to anchor there. The chances were desperate.

The ship, running right before the wind, was rushing on to the shore, and nothing could be done except round to immediately under a heavy press of canvas, and get the anchors out. Chains were hurried up from below and bent on to the anchors, which were got outboard again, and both anchors were let go in deep water. The occasion called for nerve and promptitude, and it must have been a most exciting time, as every moment the ship was drawing nearer and nearer her peril. Fortunately, the anchors held, and the ship was saved. And what a save it was, with the rocks right close up, and the ship standing gallantly beside them. Luckily the ship held on until a shift in the wind came; the chains were then slipped, and when the time came to start not a moment was lost. But two anchors and 120 fathoms of chain were left behind – all that had been between the ship and destruction. The saving of this ship, and the fine seamanship displayed is deservedly attributed to a large extent to a very fine old boatswain – Ned Parker – a typical sailor of the Nelson Type.'[1]

Waimate was sold to G. A. Lindblom, registered in Russia and renamed *Valkyrian* in 1896. She was reported missing in Lloyd's in 1898 while on a voyage from Newcastle, New South Wales, to Iquique in Chile.

Orari The first of five sister ships, *Orari* was built by Palmer's of Newcastle-on-Tyne and registered with Lloyd's in July 1875. She was an iron ship of 1,054 gross tons and her dimensions 204 feet by 34 feet by 20 feet. During her construction she narrowly escaped disaster when she capsized. However, the report on the accident showed that the ship had, in fact, suffered no damage.

Orari completed nearly 20 voyages to New Zealand, but was not particularly notable as a pace-maker. Oddly enough, her maiden voyage was her best. Her voyage to Lyttelton took 91 days, land to land only 84 days, and she arrived on 12 January 1876. Captain Fox, according to *The Lyttelton Times*, prophesied that his ship 'would prove herself a formidable antagonist to any of the many clippers now trading in New Zealand'. The newspaper was certainly impressed; it reported, 'the saloon is elegantly decorated; for convenience of Saloon passengers there is a deck smoking house on the poop, which must have proved a great comfort to smokers'. One pas-

[1] *White Wings*, pp. 252–3.

45. *Orari* off Gravesend, July 1876. (National Maritime Museum)
46. *Orari* under sail, from a painting. (Turnbull Library)

senger, the Hon. John Hall,[1] brought out 'a box of bumble bees, but it is feared, despite the attention paid to them, they are all dead!' Other livestock included sheep, cattle, a pig taken aboard at Tristan da Cunha, an Alderney cow, a Berkshire boar and Romney and Lincoln rams. The account is summed up with the statement that *Orari* 'certainly bears most favourable comparison with any vessel which has arrived in our harbour'.

The outward voyage of *Orari* in 1880 is a reminder of the way ships in the days of sail could race each other across the world, leaving a port together bound for the same destination, yet not make any contact until arrival some three months later. Shaw Savill's *Trevelyan* and *Orari* sailed from Gravesend on 7 February and after being in company in the Channel saw nothing of each other until arrival in Lyttelton on 13 and 14 May respectively. On this occasion Captain Mosey, a well-known master who was subsequently much associated with the *Waimate*, was in command.

Orari was sold by the company in 1892 to J. C. Page, and her rig changed to that of a barque. Having changed hands several times after that, she was damaged by an explosion in October 1909 and had finally disappeared from Lloyd's by 1911.

[1] v. p. 112.

47. *Orari* at Port Chalmers. (Turnbull Library)

48. Captain H. Devitt, Master of *Otaki*, 1877–1881. (From *White Wings,* p. 265)

Otaki

Registered with Lloyd's one month after *Orari*, *Otaki* was almost an exact replica of her sister, although her tonnage is given as 1,053 gross tons. Her record for speed, however, was better than that of *Orari* – and indeed, her passage from Port Chalmers to London in 1877 beat all previous sailing ship records. Of the 17 round voyages she made to New Zealand, she only exceeded 100 days on three occasions.

Two of *Otaki*'s most notable voyages were accomplished in competition with Shaw Savill's ship, *Crusader*. On 31 October 1875, *Otaki* left London with 274 emigrants; *Crusader* left three hours later the same day. *Otaki* arrived at Lyttelton on 8 February 1876, covering 3,009 miles of the voyage in 12 days; astonishingly *Crusader* arrived at Lyttelton three hours after *Otaki*. As *The Lyttleton Times* noted, 'it is a very remarkable fact that the two vessels should, after a voyage of 16,000 miles, arrive in exactly the same time, and should have been, as they were, in company with each other for a few days, and then to have lost sight of each other for so long a time'. The other occasion when the two ships raced each other was homewards from

49. *Otaki* at Picton. (Turnbull Library)
50. *Otaki* under sail, from a painting. (National Maritime Museum)

51. *Otaki* at Port Chalmers. (Turnbull Library)

Port Chalmers to London in 1877. On this voyage *Otaki* beat both *Crusader* and *Rangitiki*, making the phenomenally fast run, land to land, of 63 days – beating all previous records – and *Crusader* by one day!

But it was *Otaki*'s outward voyage to Lyttelton 1880–81, which took 105 days, that perhaps produced the most dramatic incidents in the ship's history. *The Lyttelton Times* of 6 January 1881 gives a fairly full account. Off Tasmania 'the gale blew very fiercely, and the sea rose to a great height, large quantities of water breaking on board . . . [it] broke over both quarters of the vessel in a perfect deluge, filling the main deck instantly. The doors of the saloon were burst open and a tremendous flood of water rushed through, filling all the cabins to a height of four to five feet, the whole of the passengers' effects being soaked as a matter of course. In Captain Devitt's room the water made a perfect wreck, his effects being washed away, including charts, books, etc. The force of the water in his room would not be credited, unless the traces it has left were seen . . . a hat box with a hat in it had the whole of the lining torn completely out and carried away. . . .' So far as the last details are concerned, one is at a loss which to admire the more – the gullibility of the reporter or the plausibility of the raconteur! The account concludes, 'the only piece of chart left is a small scrap, not a foot square, of Lyttelton harbour. The log-book was just saved from going over the side . . . [it is] minus its cover and, of course, saturated.'

Otaki was sold by the company to Franzius Henschen and Co. of Bremen and renamed *Dr Siegert* in 1892; her rig was subsequently changed to that of a barque. Lloyd's reported her as wrecked in July 1895.

Hurunui

This ship was registered with Lloyd's in September 1875, having been built by Palmer's of Newcastle. Her dimensions were 204 feet by 34 feet by 20 feet and she was of 1,054 gross tons. By 1890, her rig had been changed to that of a barque. During her ownership by The N.Z.S. Co., *Hurunui* made nearly 20 voyages to New Zealand, but she was never a great pace-maker. Her best outward voyage was in 1895, when she reached Lyttelton in 86 days, but on several other outward voyages she took more than 100 days. Her voyage to Napier

52. *Otaki* at Queen's Wharf, Wellington. (Turnbull Library)

in 1892 took no less than 125 days, of which more than a month was spent repairing in Capetown! Self-entertainment was a most necessary feature of these long periods at sea, and *The Lyttelton Times* reporting on a long voyage in December 1879 rather pompously noted that 'concerts, oceanic minstrels' performances and other shipboard pastimes were held on thoroughly orthodox principles, being under the patronage and in the presence of the most esteemed Commander'.

One of the most exciting incidents in *Hurunui*'s career was her passage through Alderney Race, the strait separating the island of Alderney from Normandy, in the face of a hurricane in December 1893. The occasion has been vividly described: 'In stormy weather this strait is a fearsome place. If you look at the chart you will see three-and-a-half and four fathom patches, numerous rocks, and to complicate matters there is a furious tide of anything from four to six-and-a-half knots. Imagine this turbulent spot on a mid-winter's night, the *Hurunui* laden right down to her marks! There were breakers everywhere, and the ship's decks were full of water to the rails half the time. With two men at the wheel, two lower topsails and the foresail set, the ship had a most nerve-wracking experience, and the wonder is that she lived through it all. Three of her four boats were badly smashed, the only one to escape being the fourth, which was high up in the poop davits.'[1]

Even after negotiating the Alderney Race, *Hurunui*'s troubles were not at an end for, continuing her passage down the Channel, she narrowly escaped running down a small coaster, which had started to leak in the storm, and whose ballast had shifted. Three men were aboard the wreck and these were with some difficulty picked up by the *Hurunui*'s boat.

Ten years previously, in 1883, *Hurunui* had been involved in another fearsome incident in the English Channel. This was her collision with the first ship owned by the company – *Waitara* – which resulted in the sinking of the latter with loss of life.[2]

Perhaps in New Zealand the most remembered incident of *Hurunui*'s career was the opening of Lyttelton Graving Dock in January 1883. The occasion is well recorded by a number of excel-

[1] *White Wings*, p. 259.
[2] v. pp. 47–8.

53. *Hurunui* opening Lyttelton Graving Dock, January 1883. (London Office)

54. *Hurunui* at Port Chalmers. (Turnbull Library)
55. *Hurunui* under sail, from a painting. (Turnbull Library)

lent photographs. *The Lyttelton Times* of 4 January sets the scene: 'The ship, which was the very perfection of neatness and order, was dressed in real holiday style, an arc of flags extending from the jib-boom end over her masts to the end of her gaff.' The ship was drawing 14 feet aft and 13 feet 6 inches forward. The acting Governor, Sir James Prendergast, gave Captain Haselwood a gold pencil case and said that he congratulated 'the Captain on being the Commander of the first ship to enter the Dock, and considered that the fact that one of N.Z.S. Co.'s ships being the first vessel in this Dock must be most satisfactory to everyone. The N.Z.S. Co. possessed a fleet of ships which for beauty of design, comfort of passengers, and skill of their commanders could not be surpassed by any company.'

In 1895 *Hurunui* was sold to J. Lindblom, and was renamed *Hermes*, under the Russian flag. She survived another 20 years, being sunk in April 1915 by a German submarine having changed ownership although retaining Russian registration.

57. *Hurunui* opening Lyttelton Graving Dock, January 1883. (Turnbull Library)

56. *Hurunui* at Port Chalmers. (Turnbull Library)

CANTERBURY NEW ZEALAND

LYTTELTON HARBOUR BOARD

CELEBRATION OF DOCK OPENING

JANUARY 3RD 1883.

MENU

WINES

WINES

WHITE BURGUNDY

Spg Red do.

WHITE BORDEAUX.

Sauterne
Barsac

HOCK.

Laubenheim
Rudesheim
Steinberg Cabinet
Schloss Johannisberg (*vin.* 1868)
Spg. Johannisberger

CLARET.

Château Brane Cantenac
Château Margaux, grand vin (*vin.* 1870)
Château Lafite grand vin (*vint.* 1877) (Magnums)
Château Lafite grand vin (*vint.* 1876) (Jeroboam)

CHAMPAGNE.

Jules Mumm (Magnums)
Veuve Clicquot Ponsardin "dry"
Heidsieck dry Monopole
Pommery, "extra sec."

SOUPS

Clear Italian   White Oyster

JOINTS.

Roast Sirloin of Beef
Roast Lamb
Roast Saddle Mutton, Red Currant Jelly

POULTRY.

Galantine of Turkey Truffles
Galantine of Chicken

Galantine of Veal

ROAST.

Wild Ducks   Chickens
Ducks

BOILED

Corned Beef   Hams   Tongues
Mayonnaise of Salmon
Mayonnaise of Trout

VEGETABLES IN SEASON.

SWEETS.

Italian Cream   Orange Jelly
Merangues   Queen Mab Pudding
Trifles   Golden Jelly
Compot of Peaches
Charlotte aux Pommes
Tartlets   Cream

DESSERT

Hot-house Grapes   Strawberries
Plums   Pears   Apples
Pine Apples   Oranges

SHERRY.

Fine Old Dry Pale

Finest Old Amontillado

Finest Old Vino de Paste

Finest Old Gold

PORT.

Very Finest Old White

Finest Old Red

MADEIRA.

Finest Old East India (Bot. 1872)

LIQUEURS.

Otard's Brandy (*vin.* 1848)

Benedictine

Curacoa

J.W.T.Boys. Del.

J. BUGGEY CATERER.

58. Menu for a banquet given by Lyttelton Harbour Board in celebration of the opening of the new dock by *Hurunui,* January 1883 – a magnificent repast in spite of some eccentric spelling! (Christchurch Boardroom)

Waipa

Registered with Lloyd's one month after *Hurunui*, *Waipa* was an exact sister ship, except that her tonnage is given as 1,057 gross tons. She made nearly 20 voyages to New Zealand under the flag of The N.Z.S. Co., but was not renowned for her speedy passages. One of her best outward voyages was to Port Chalmers in 1875, when she accomplished a land to land time of 82 days. *The Otago Daily Times* of 1 November 1879 reported: 'The good ship comes into port a pattern of neatness and good order, and reflects the very greatest credit both on the Commander (the genial Captain Gorn) and his indefatigable chief officer, Mr. J. Baxter. She brings 1,500 tons of cargo, of which 200 tons are deadweight, and the rest measurement goods.

59. *Waipa* at Port Chalmers. (Turnbull Library)

She had also 1,000 birds, the survivors of 1,600 collected by their owner from various parts of Europe. He informs us that out of 120 insectivorous birds, only 12 survived, of these two are nightingales and the remainder robins. . . . The *Waipa* also brings a cow. This docile creature is in full milk and has, of course, been duly appreciated by the passengers.'

Births, marriages and deaths not infrequently, of course, occurred during the long haul of more than three months between England and New Zealand in the days of the sailing ships. Surely one of the most remarkable christenings of all was celebrated aboard *Waipa*

60. *Waipa* at Port Chalmers. (Turnbull Library)

when a child was given the names 'Cyclone Four Bells Cape Dove Gorn Bendall Waipa . . .', all of which were duly returned on the Board of Trade form. The explanation is fairly obvious, the infant was born in a cyclone at four bells off Cape Dove, *Waipa*'s doctor being named Bendall and her Master, Captain Gorn!

The testimony of the journal of the Surgeon-Superintendent, C. H. Gibson, made after the voyage to Wellington in 1876, gives perhaps the most fitting summary of *Waipa* and her owners: 'The general arrangements of The N.Z.S. Co. in my opinion (after an experience of five years at sea as surgeon) contrast most favourably with those of other companies.'

Waipa was sold in 1895 to Brodrene Bjornstad, Norwegian owners, and renamed *Munter*; her rig was later changed to that of a barque. She lasted until December 1911, when Lloyd's reported her as 'missing'.

The last of the five sister ships to be built by Palmer's of Newcastle, *Wairoa* was registered with Lloyd's in November 1875. Her dimensions were 204 feet by 34 feet by 20 feet and she was of 1,057 gross tons. Her arrival in Canterbury on her maiden voyage was well reported upon by *The Lyttelton Times*, which in its issue of 29 June 1876, said 'in every respect [she is] a really magnificent vessel. Her spars appear to be somewhat lighter than those of the *Waipa*, which certainly adds much to her appearance aloft where everything seemed in fine order. . . . She has logged 315 miles in 24 hours. . . . [On passage the] condenser broke down, and she put into the Cape for water. . . . The accommodation is well lighted and ventilated, besides being very roomy.' In spite of these early eulogies on this 'fast sailer', *Wairoa*'s later record is not one of quick passages. Out of nearly 20 voyages to New Zealand she took 100 days or more on nine occasions. One of her longest voyages was to Wellington in 1879, when she took 108 days – spending nearly three weeks in the Doldrums. On arrival in New Zealand, she suffered further delay since many children had developed measles and the ship was placed in quarantine. In 1894, on her last voyage for the company, *Wairoa* was in competition homewards with Shaw Savill's very fast clipper *Westland*. This ship held

Wairoa

61. *Wairoa* being towed to Dunedin. The funnel amidships belongs to the second tug. (Turnbull Library)

the record for the outward voyage to Dunedin, 66 days land to land, which was the same time as *Waimate*'s record to Lyttelton achieved in 1881. *Wairoa* sailed from Bluff an hour before *Westland* and took 91 days to get home, which was not an uncreditable performance. As she arrived, however, she encountered *Westland* having completed discharge and loading being towed out of the dock on her next outward voyage from London.

Wairoa's best voyage, however, was to Port Chalmers in 1893 when she took 90 days (86 days land to land). *The Otago Daily Times* graciously summed up her appearance – 'The *Wairoa* comes into port in most beautiful order'.

Wairoa was sold in 1895 to C. Zernichow and O. Gotaas, Norwegian owners, and renamed *Winnipeg*. Her rig was subsequently altered to that of a barque. Later, having changed to Russian ownership, she left Pensacola, USA, with a lumber cargo for Buenos Aires and was reported 'missing' in Lloyd's in December 1907.

62. *Wairoa* in dry dock in London. (National Maritime Museum)

Opawa *Opawa* was the first of three sister ships to be built for the company by Stephen's of Glasgow, being registered with Lloyd's in November 1876; the others were *Piako* and *Wanganui*. These three were the last sailing ships to be built specially for the company. She was an iron ship of 1,131 gross tons and her dimensions were 215 feet by 34 feet by 20 feet. *Opawa* had the reputation of being a good pace-maker and out of a total of more than 20 voyages to New Zealand she accomplished seven in less than 90 days. Her best voyage was in 1880 when she reached Lyttelton in 81 days with 197 passengers aboard. *The Lyttelton Times* of 27 October patronisingly describes them as 'an exceptionally respectable body of people'. The appearance of the ship herself also received praise – 'the accommodation [being] scrupulously neat and clean'. The voyage outwards had been a remarkable one, for in the Channel the passengers had seen 'an unusual and grand sight' – 11 English warships. The Master, Captain Triston, had at first been alarmed, having obtained no sights for two days and, 'seeing only the tops of their top-gallant masts above the water thought that they were trees on an island, as the weather was not very clear. The *Opawa* stood across the bows of the fleet, affording her passengers a splendid view of the very rare and grand sight. The decks of the men of war . . . were crowded with blue jackets, all anxious to have a look at the number of fair passengers [*Opawa*] had aboard!'

The outward voyage to Wellington of 1884–85 was notable for the tragedy which befell *Opawa*'s Master, Captain Mathers. One evening, after having complained of an ailment for some days, he walked towards the forecastle and attempted to jump overboard, but was prevented. Shortly after, he leapt over the starboard side, and although the ship was hove-to and the body recovered within ten minutes, Captain Mathers was dead. *The Evening Post* tells us 'no reason can be assigned for his jumping overboard, but it is believed that the illness had deranged his mind'. The ship was brought on by Mr Banks, the chief officer, 'a gentleman long and favourably known in Wellington'.

Opawa was sold in 1899 to S. O. Stray and took Norwegian registration, being renamed *Aquila*. She survived under her new name, in Lloyd's, until 1918–19.

63. *Opawa* at Port Chalmers. (Turnbull Library)
64. *Opawa* in London. The funnel of the refrigeration machinery appears
prominently on deck. (National Maritime Museum)

Piako A sister ship of *Opawa* and *Wanganui*, *Piako* was built by Stephen's of Glasgow, and registered with Lloyd's in December 1876. Her dimensions were 215 feet by 34 feet by 21 feet and she was of 1,136 gross tons. Her best voyage to New Zealand was in 1878 when she took $76\frac{1}{2}$ days from Plymouth to Port Chalmers; but of her 17 outward voyages, five exceeded 100 days. The name of *Piako* is, however, probably most associated with two memorable fires at sea. The second, and less fearful occasion, occurred on Christmas morning 1879, when a case of rockets in the storeroom exploded and a large quantity of smoke issued from the after hatch. The scene was reported in *The Lyttelton Times* which concludes, 'the fire hoses were at once got down the 'tween decks and the fire eventually subdued without any serious damage'.

The far more dramatic and nearly tragic fire took place on the outward voyage in 1878. *Piako* had set sail from England with 1,050 tons of cargo and 288 emigrants, and was about 200 miles off Pernambuco, Brazil. *The Lyttelton Times* gives us a graphic account of

65. *Piako* off Gravesend, 3 February 1877. (National Maritime Museum)

the disaster as it must have been reported by the ship's officers on their eventual arrival in New Zealand nearly four months later. At 10.45 a.m. on 11 November, the chief officer had run into the master's cabin, and reported that smoke was issuing from the lower fore hatch. Within six minutes of this, 'Captain Boyd distinctly saw a flame about 20 feet abaft the foremost tier of cargo . . . huge volumes of black sulphurous smoke were soon belching from the ship in spite of wet blankets being spread over everything and hoses applied'. 'For half an hour or so after it was known that the matter was really serious', wrote a passenger afterwards,[1] 'there was a tremendous rushing about; the men excited and the women whimpering; but seeing the Captain display such courage, and hearing him tell us we would be right enough, kept everybody in good spirits. He was simply grand. There he stood right on the railing of the poop, stripped to his shirt and trousers, a loaded revolver in his hand, shouting out his orders.' Four hours after the start of the fire, and seeing

[1] *White Wings*, pp. 270–2.

66. *Piako* under sail, from a painting. (Turnbull Library)

the peril in which his ship was placed, the master ordered all the boats out, but about two p.m. much to the relief of everyone a barque, *Loch Doon*, was sighted. Contact was made and eventually all the passengers were transferred from the burning ship. Captain Boyd then told his crew 'he intended if possible to take the ship into port, and every man on board said that he would, and did, stick to the ship; and right manfully they worked, never leaving the pumps till four p.m. on 13 November'. On arrival at Pernambuco, it was necessary to scuttle the *Piako* – 'smoking and blazing up to the moment she was submerged. Of the ship's cargo nothing that was perishable was saved; in fact so great was the heat in the lower hold, that crates of bottles and galvanised iron were fused, and afterwards taken out of the ship in great lumps and cakes.' Even arrival at Pernambuco was not the end of the discomfort, for a smallpox epidemic was raging there, and people were dying at the rate of 400 per day. Captain Boyd, on discovering this, hired an island some seven miles up the river, called Cocoanut Island, where the emigrants were installed for six weeks, in a makeshift camp of huts of bamboo canes and leaves.[1] At the Naval Court of Enquiry held at Pernambuco, Captain Boyd and his officers and crew were, with good reason, 'complimented on their brave and meritorious conduct under very trying circumstances'. *Piako*, after being raised and refitted, eventually arrived in New Zealand 145 days after leaving England.

In spite of the drama of this particular voyage, it is perhaps more pleasant to recall *Piako* in the words of *The Otago Daily Times* of February 1878. She is 'one of the handsomest of The N.Z.S. Co.'s clippers and has a neat and cleanly appearance alow and aloft'.

Piako was sold in 1892 to E. Shaeffer, German owners. Lloyd's finally reported her missing in November 1900, when bound, it is said, from Melbourne to the Cape with supplies for the troops in the Boer War.[2]

[1] Extracts from a diary kept by R. A. Bayliffe on this eventful voyage were printed in *Crossed Flags*, The N.Z.S. Co's house journal, No. 3, pp. 19–23 and No. 4, pp. 25–9, 1966.

[2] In the Altonaer Museum, in Hamburg, there is a figurehead in the form of a Red Indian, which purports to have belonged to *Piako*. This ascription seems at least doubtful in view of the fact that *Piako* was apparently lost at sea and it is not likely that the original figurehead was ever removed even when she changed ownership. Further, the subject of a Red Indian seems an unlikely one for a ship built for The N.Z.S. Co. Unfortunately, the photographs of the ship which exist do not assist in deciding the matter.

V. *Opawa*, oil painting by G. H. Elvin. (London Office)

67. *Wanganui* at Port Chalmers. The ship's figurehead was carved in the likeness of the Chairman's wife, Mrs J. L. Coster. (Turnbull Library)

The last of the three sister ships built by Stephen's of Glasgow and the last sailing ship to be built specifically for the company, *Wanganui* was registered with Lloyd's in January 1877. She was of 1,136 gross tons and her dimensions were 215 feet by 34 feet by 20 feet. Her figurehead was carved in the likeness of Mrs J. L. Coster, the wife of the company's Chairman! *Wanganui*'s career was fairly uneventful, and she was better known for her fine appearance than her speed. Indeed, out of nearly 20 voyages to New Zealand, not all of which were under The N.Z.S. Co.'s flag, more than half took more than 100 days. Her best outward voyage was one of her earliest – she arrived in New Zealand after a passage of 80 days. *The Lyttleton*

Wanganui

68. *Wanganui* under sail, from a painting. (Turnbull Library)

Times of 13 February 1878 reported upon her appearance. *Wanganui* 'arrived in splendid order everywhere and in good trim', there had been 'no lack of excellent provisions and not a complaint throughout the ship'. On one day during the outward passage, she had sailed 330 miles. The 241 immigrants on board looked remarkably well and as though they would be a 'useful class of people for the colony'. *Wanganui*'s second best outward voyage occurred the following year, and *The Otago Daily Times* of 8 December 1879 provided the eulogy on that occasion: 'That the ship is eminently calculated for passengers is undeniable, her lofty 'tween decks and perfect system of ventilation being all that could be desired. The ship comes into port in first-rate condition ... while the parts allotted for passengers are perfect models of cleanliness and good order. Indeed, we have never seen a vessel come into port in such a state of cleanliness and comfort as did the *Wanganui*. In order to keep [the passengers] occupied, boat and fire drill were strictly observed, concerts were held and divine service [also] strictly observed'. The account condescendingly concludes, the 'passengers are a very respectable class of people and appear to be well fitted to become settled residents amongst us'.

Wanganui was sold in 1888 to J. Leslie of Aberdeen, an associate of Shaw Savill and Co., and renamed *Blenheim*. She had been transferred to H. C. A. Michelsen by 1904 and subsequently went through several other changes in Norwegian ownership before she finally disappeared from Lloyd's in 1917 – after a career of 40 years.

Pareora (ex White Eagle)

This ship was built in 1855 in Glasgow for Messrs Stephen and McFarlan. Her dimensions were approximately 203 feet by 33 feet by 21 feet and she was an iron ship of 879 gross tons. The N.Z.S. Co. acquired her in April 1877; her name was changed in the following September. Of all the sailing ships owned by the company this was the earliest in point of construction, dating as she did from the period of the Crimean War. *Pareora* accomplished 12 voyages to New Zealand, two of them before she was under the company's flag. In 1881 she was almost lost on her outward voyage from London to Auckland. While she was anchored in the Downs, a terrific gale blew up and *Pareora* was driven from her moorings. She received some damage but after returning to Gravesend set sail again for New Zealand on a voyage which was to take 110 days.

Pareora's best voyage was in 1883, when she reached Port Chalmers in 83 days, 72 days land to land, which was considered a great achievement for a small ship that was nearly 30 years old. She arrived, in the words of *The Otago Daily Times*, 'in splendid order and reflects great credit on the Captain and officers'. She carried 1,800 tons of cargo and 21 passengers 'all of whom have enjoyed excellent health'. Another fairly fast voyage occurred in 1894, when *Pareora* arrived in Auckland in 94 days. *The New Zealand Herald* tells us that there were tremendous gales in the Indian Ocean and 'mountainous sea broke freely over the deck, the saloon was flooded, the steering apparatus carried away and several sails lost . . . she shipped several seas which filled the cabins, deck houses and everything else and a portion of the bulwarks was carried away'. The cargo was valued at £34,800 and included such miscellaneous items as 100 barrels of gunpowder, four cases of night lights, 30 cases of sardines, two cases of Venetian blinds, 11 cases of sausage machines, 30 copper furnace boilers, 20 sets of wagon wheels and three cases of patent water-closets!

Pareora was sold in 1887 by The N.Z.S. Co. to J. Livingston, but within two years, according to Lloyd's, she had been broken up.

69. *Pareora* at Port Chalmers. (Turnbull Library)

Built in 1868 by C. Connell and Co. of Glasgow, the *City of Perth* was an iron ship of 1,247 gross tons. Her dimensions were 233 feet by 35 feet by 22 feet. Her early years were spent in the ownership of Smith and Sons' City Line operating in the Indian trade. The events which led to her being purchased by The N.Z.S. Co. are dramatic.[1] The *City of Perth* was loading in Timaru on 15 May 1882 when some tremendous seas, whipped up by a gale, started to play havoc with the ships lying in the roadstead. The cables of one of them, the *Ben Venue*, parted and her crew abandoned her and went aboard

Turakina (ex City of Perth)

[1] *White Wings*, pp. 129–31.

70. *City of Perth* (later *Turakina*) and *Ben Venue* aground in Caroline Bay, Timaru, in 1882. (Turnbull Library)

the *City of Perth*. This was not before time, for the *Ben Venue* was rapidly driven ashore and became a total wreck. Meanwhile, the *City of Perth* was also clearly getting into difficulties and the crew took to the boats and got safely ashore. The Harbourmaster then went out to the *City of Perth* followed by two other boats; but at this moment the last remaining hawser holding the ship parted and she drifted right on to the shore. By this time 'the line of breakers were rolling like mountains, white with foam'. In turn all three boats capsized in the terrific sea; the lifeboat was then launched from the shore and this itself capsized three times before bringing back most of the victims to safety. Although the *Ben Venue* was a total loss, the *City of Perth* was later refloated and repaired and was bought by The N.Z.S. Co.; she was re-registered with her new name in Lloyd's

71. *Turakina* at Port Chalmers. (Turnbull Library)

72. Captain Power, Master of *Turakina*. (From *White Wings*, p. 131)

in April 1883. The last to be acquired, *Turakina* was the largest of the company's sailing ships.

Turakina had several other notable experiences of foul weather. In 1888 outward bound the chief officer and a seaman were washed overboard and drowned. Ten years later, in 1898, again on the outward passage, 'all the skylights, poop rails, top gallant rails and bulwarks were swept overboard . . .'. The ship laboured heavily and it was found necessary to lash the men to the wheel in order to keep the ship steady, while oil bags were constantly kept out both fore and aft.[1] The ship was eventually forced to put into Algoa Bay for repairs. The outward voyage on this occasion took 191 days! Her cargo, according to *The Otago Daily Times*, included eight anvils, 36 axle arms, 409 cases of beer, 31 bundles of bedsteads, 12 bellows, 50 grindstones, 50 boxes of candles and 2,100 sash weights. On yet another occasion, this time homeward bound, *Turakina* encountered many large icebergs in the South Atlantic so that 'it seemed certain she must go ashore'.

[1] *White Wings*, p. 131.

South Atlantic Dangers

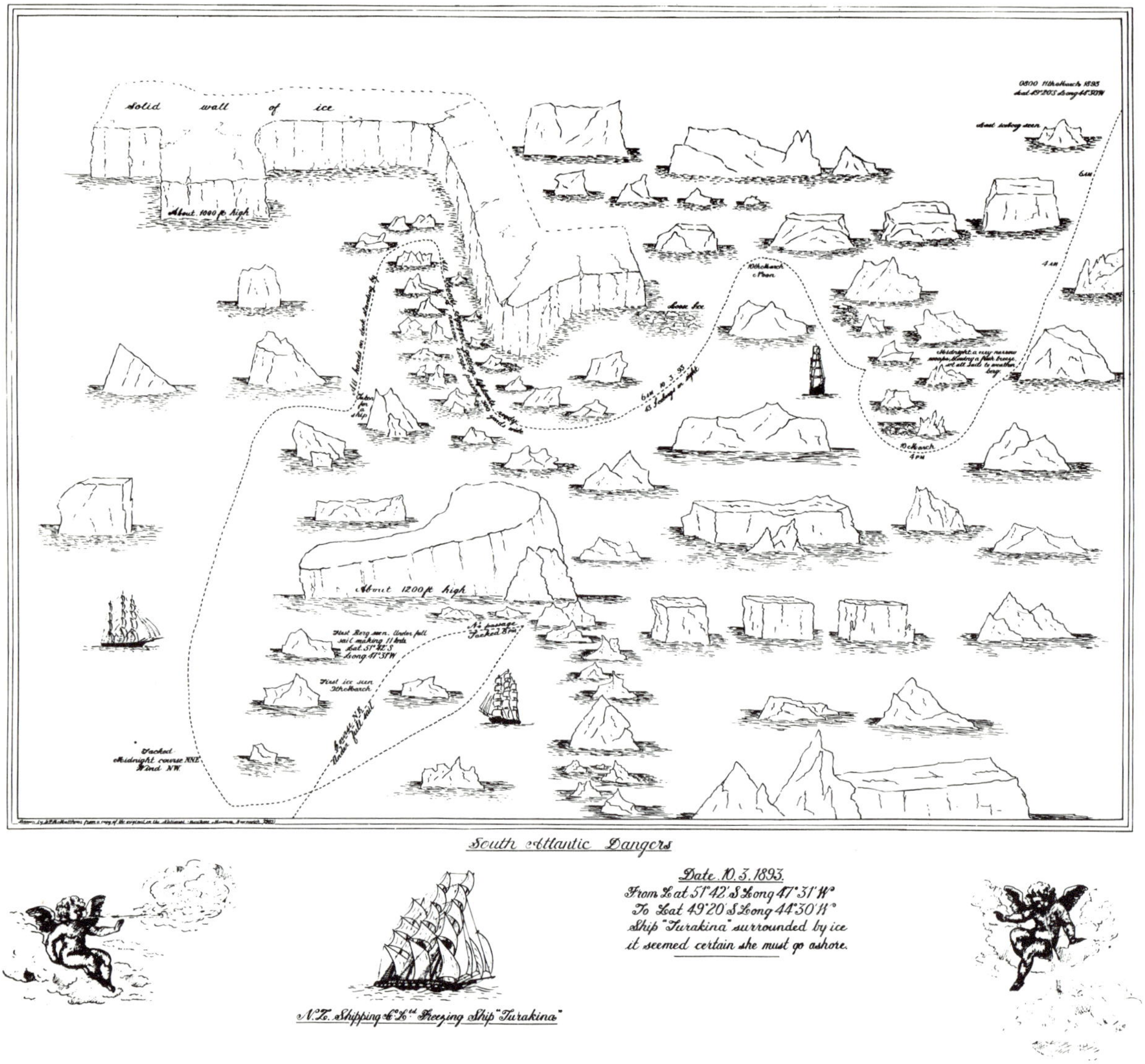

Date 10.3.1893.
From Lat 51°42′S Long 47°31′W
To Lat 49°20′S Long 44°30′W
Ship "Turakina" surrounded by ice
it seemed certain she must go ashore.

N.Z. Shipping Co.s Freezing Ship "Turakina"

73. 'South Atlantic Dangers', *Turakina*'s passage through the ice, 10 March 1893. (National Maritime Museum)

Although *Turakina* never succeeded in breaking her record of 83 days on an outward leg she was a consistently fast pace-maker taking less than 90 days on seven out of her 15 voyages to New Zealand. But it was on 14 February 1895 that *Turakina* achieved her most famous feat of speed – overhauling the company's steamer *Ruapehu*. It is said that on this occasion *Turakina* covered the 5,000 miles be-

T. Ruddiman Johnston   Murrayfield Edinburgh

74. Map of New Zealand. This is reproduced from *New Zealand, its history, institutions and industries* by 'A Resident', which was compiled for The N.Z.S. Co. in 1884. (Turnbull Library)

tween the meridians of the Cape and Leeuwin in 16 days, her best run being 308. The eye-witness account of *Ruapehu*'s fourth officer, B. C. D'Arcy Maxwell, tells the story: 'I was fourth officer of the RMS *Ruapehu* in the year 1895. We were running the Easting down on a voyage from Cape Town to Hobart, Tasmania, thence to New Zealand and in approx. Lat. 46° South I went on the bridge at 9 a.m. and relieved the third officer (Mr E. J. Tosswill) for breakfast. The master (Capt. Findlay) came on the bridge almost immediately after, and asked me if anything was in sight (in customary habit). I replied "No, Sir". With that I scanned the horizon right round and observed an object away astern on the starboard quarter, and reported it to him. The master said "A damn fine lookout you're keeping", thinking it was a vessel that had passed going in the opposite direction. I answered "Sir, I am looking out ahead and have only just taken over from the third officer." We were steering about due East, the wind N.W. freshening, and we carried on the foremast foresail, topsail, top gallant sail, staysail and trysail and on the main mast – main topsail, top gallant sail, staysail and trysail, which aiding our steam-driven power gave us a speed of about 14 knots through the water. The ship, which proved to be the company's own sailing ship *Turakina*, rapidly came up on us, and a magnificent sight she was with all sail set, heeling over to the freshening wind, when at noon she was abeam of us close to leeward. Her Master (Capt. J. Hamon) could be clearly seen excitedly waving to us from the poop weather rail, the ships' respective crew and passengers hailing each other as the *Turakina* drew ahead. By this time the *Ruapehu*'s engines had been opened out, and she was logging $14\frac{1}{2}$ knots, but the *Turakina* swept past us, and at 1 p.m. crossed our bows, surely as notable a feat of its kind as ever a Seaman dared. Then having weathered us and accomplished his intention Captain Hamon found it necessary to shorten sail, the wind increasing in force, and in doing so the *Turakina* gradually dropped back on the weather beam, until at sunset she was away on the weather quarter having reduced down to a main topgallant sail.

'On our arrival in Wellington, N.Z., this incident was duly inserted in the newspapers as one of the events of the voyage, which was the custom in the old days. About a week later the *Turakina* arrived in port, and whilst at dinner, the evening of that day, Captain Hamon (a Jerseyman) came excitedly into the Saloon, calling out (in his broken English) "Captain, Captain, you tell them that in Lat. and Long. so and so you pass me. No Sir, you not pass me – I pass you! ! !" much to the intense amusement of us all. After acknowledging this fact and complimenting him on his unique feat, Captain Hamon (and his ship) were duly toasted, and this ended a very memorable incident of "Sail versus Steam".'

Turakina was sold in 1899 to Norwegian owners who shortly afterwards renamed her *Elida*; her rig was later changed to that of a barque. Lloyd's reported her as 'broken up' in May 1914.

Appendix I

*The Directors of
The New Zealand
Shipping Co., Ltd.
1873–1970*

The following information has generally been compiled from the lists of the management of the company which are displayed at the beginning of each Annual Report. For the sake of uniformity, it has been assumed throughout that each list refers to the financial year under review. It should be appreciated therefore that since the dates given below refer to the financial years concerned, it is possible that, occasionally, appointment or resignation actually occurred in the calendar year preceding or following the one recorded.

Since the company's first Annual Report was not, of course, issued until 1874, the names of the Directors who were appointed at the foundation of the company in 1873 have been extracted from the Board minutes. Likewise, since all the copies of the Annual Reports for the years between 1919 and 1929 seem to have disappeared, recourse has had to be made to the respective Board minutes in London and New Zealand to complete the list of Directors in these years.

Certain biographical details about the early Chairmen and Directors of the company are given in the Introduction. Further information is given about certain other Directors – more particularly those of the sailing ship era – in the footnotes below. For the New Zealand Directors these details have been mostly drawn from *A Dictionary of New Zealand Biography* edited by G. H. Scholefield (Wellington, 1940). The appropriate editions of *Who's Who* have also provided some useful information about some of the Directors on both the New Zealand and London Boards.

Some of the company's Directors have been members of Parliament or knighted during or after their service on the Board. Such distinctions are recorded below, although they do not necessarily relate to the period of the Directors' membership of the Board. The following symbols are used to denote the distinctions indicated:

† a Member of the House of Representatives
* a Member of the Legislative Council
‡ a Member of Parliament.

John Lewis Coster, 1873–1874, 1875–1886†
William Reeves, 1874–1875†*
Hugh Percy Murray-Aynsley, 1886–1887,[1] 1893–1916†
Leonard Harper, 1889–1892†
Arthur Edgar Gravenor Rhodes, 1917–1921†[2]
John Anderson, 1922[3]
George Gould, 1923–1940[4]
Sir Robert Albert Anderson, C.M.G., 1941[5]
Charles Murray Turrell, 1942–1944
John Deans, 1944–1962
Derrick William Joseph Gould, 1963–   [4]

Board of Directors

John Lewis Coster, 1873–1886†
John Thomas Peacock, 1873–1881†*[6]
Reginald Cobb, 1873[7]
John Anderson, 1873–1897[8]

[1] For much of the crisis of 1887–88 (v. pp. 36–7) – Murray-Aynsley having resigned in December 1887 – 'the Director on rota took the chair at the weekly meetings of the Board and was consulted on all matters during his term of office'. (Annual Report, November 1888.)

[2] After taking his degree at Cambridge and being called to the Bar, he returned to New Zealand. He was, at various times, Chairman of the Christchurch Press Co. Ltd. and of the Board of Governors of Canterbury College. He was also Mayor of Christchurch.

[3] He was a son of John Anderson, who was a Director on the New Zealand Board 1873–1897 (q.v.).

[4] v. p. 110, note 2.

[5] He was Managing Director of J. G. Ward and Co., Ltd., Invercargill. He was also Chairman of Nestlé and Anglo-Swiss Condensed Milk Co. (Australasia), Ltd. and of New Zealand Milk Products, Ltd.

[6] A Canterbury merchant, he represented Lyttelton in Parliament and was Chairman of its Harbour Board.

[7] He represented the New Zealand Loan and Mercantile Agency Co., Ltd., one of the major original promoters of the company (v. p. 11, note 1).

[8] An early Canterbury settler, he was by trade a blacksmith; his forge in Christchurch and the Canterbury ironworks which developed from it so prospered that by the 1880s Anderson was building boilers, constructing railways and launching his first steam ship at Lyttelton. His son (q.v.) succeeded him as a Director of The N.Z.S. Co.

R. H. Rhodes, 1873–1874[1]

George Gould, 1873[2]

William Reeves, 1873–1881†*

John Studholme, 1873–1902†[3]

Samuel S. Revans, 1873–1879

John Johnston, 1873–1885*[4]

Sir John Logan Campbell, 1873–1889†[5]

Evan Prosser, 1873–1876[6]

Charles Wesley Turner, 1875–1880

Hugh Percy Murray-Aynsley, 1875–1916†

Alexander Cracroft Wilson, 1875–1890

Robert Campbell, 1877–1887†*[7]

Edward Richardson, C.M.G., 1880–1914†*[8]

[1] A prosperous farmer and philanthropist; he donated the tower and peal of eight bells to Christchurch Cathedral.

[2] Born in England, he emigrated to New Zealand in 1850. He became engaged in many commercial undertakings in Christchurch, where he was a considerable philanthropist. He was a founder of the company which was to be called Pyne, Gould, Guinness, Ltd. His brother Joseph, son George, and grandson D. W. J. Gould (q.v.) were all to become Directors on the New Zealand Board.

[3] A pioneering farmer of the more adventurous type, he once walked from Nelson to Bluff. He was one of the first Europeans to travel overland from Christchurch to Dunedin.

[4] He was a member of the Legislative Council for 29 years.

[5] After obtaining his M.D. at Edinburgh University, he went out to Australia in 1839 and crossed to New Zealand the following year. He was one of the founding fathers of Auckland, of which he was later a distinguished benefactor. In 1844 he and his partner, William Brown, loaded the barque *Bolina* with what was reputed to be the first cargo of New Zealand produce for the English market.

[6] A chemist and druggist by training, he was involved in the gold discoveries in Westland in the 1860s. He was Mayor of Hokitika in 1868. He later settled in Dunedin. He was one of the founders of the firm of Kempthorne, Prosser and Co. Ltd.

[7] Educated at Eton, he emigrated to New Zealand in the 1860s. A Canterbury farmer, he represented Oamaru in Parliament and also served on its Harbour Board. Campbell's name is omitted from the list of Directors in the Annual Report of 1883, but there is no reference in the Report to his resignation or in the 1884 Report to his re-election although he does appear in the list of Directors for the latter year and in every subsequent year until 1888. It has therefore been assumed that the omission of his name for 1883 was an error.

[8] A civil engineer by training, he went out to New Zealand in 1861 under contract to construct the Christchurch/Lyttelton railway. He later represented Christchurch city in Parliament and became Minister of Public Works.

Robert Wilkin, 1881–1885†[1]
Henry John Tancred, 1883†*[2]
Leonard Harper, 1885–1892†
Sir Charles Christopher Bowen, K.C.M.G, 1886–1917†*[3]
Percy John Fryer, 1887–1904
J. R. Blair, 1888–1914[4]
Joseph Gould, 1890–1903[5]
Arthur Edgar Gravenor Rhodes, 1896–1921†[6]
G. G. Stead, 1898–1907[7]
John Anderson, 1898–1934[8]
F. de C. Malet, 1903–1911[9]
Sir George Hugh Charles Clifford, Bart., 1904–1930[10]
George Gould, 1905–1940[11]
F. H. Pyne, 1909–1915
William Reece, 1913–1930[12]
Sir Charles John Johnston, 1915–1917†*[13]

[1] He was a Canterbury run-holder and stock and station agent.

[2] Educated at Rugby under Arnold, he served for some time in a hussar regiment of the Austrian army. He arrived in New Zealand in 1850; a friend of Godley, he was a prominent member of the Canterbury Association. Tancred held several portfolios in various governments, including that of Postmaster-General. He was the first Chancellor of the University of New Zealand.

[3] Educated at Rugby and Cambridge, he arrived in Lyttelton in 1850 with his parents aboard the *Charlotte Jane*. For two years he was private secretary to Godley, the virtual governor, and later serving as inspector of police he had to do his part in the apprehension and prosecution of the notorious James MacKenzie for sheep-stealing.

[4] He was the first Chairman of the Bank of New Zealand and Mayor of Wellington 1878–1879.

[5] v. p. 110, note 2.

[6] v. p. 109, note 2.

[7] He was Chairman of the Christchurch Press Co. Ltd.

[8] v. p. 109, note 8.

[9] A barrister, he was Chairman of the Board of Governors of Canterbury College and government Director of the Bank of New Zealand.

[10] Keenly interested in sheep-breeding and racing, he won all the leading races in the Dominion – most of them on several occasions. He was the son of Sir Charles Clifford, the first baronet, a Director on the London Board (q.v.).

[11] v. p. 110, note 2.

[12] A hardware merchant, he was a Director of several Christchurch companies and was Mayor of the city in 1900.

[13] He was a member of the Legislative Council for more than 25 years and was Speaker for a period. He was the son of John Johnston who was a Director on the New Zealand Board (q.v.).

Arthur William Bennett, 1920–1930
John Henry Casson Bond, 1926–1932
Sir Robert Albert Anderson, C.M.G., 1928–1941[1]
Joseph Francis Studholme, 1930
Col. John Studholme, C.B.E., D.S.O., 1931–1934[2]
Charles Murray Turrell, 1933–1944
Sir Charles Lewis Clifford, Bart., 1934[3]
Arthur Ernest Cooper, 1934–1937
Arthur Sims, 1938–1943
John Deans, 1938–1962
Thomas James Maling, 1940–1951
Ebenezer Hay, 1942
Donald Sinclair Murchison, D.S.O., 1943–1969
Derrick William Joseph Gould, 1943–
Humphrey Holderness, 1946–1951
Francis William Spite, 1946–1962
Derek Skene Studholme, M.B.E., 1952–
Thomas Sidney Marchington, D.S.C., 1959–1967
Harold Herbert Elworthy, 1960–
Frederick Reed Alan Hellaby, 1960–
Sir Edward Denis Blundell, K.B.E., 1966–1967[4]
Gray Hunter, 1966–
Peter Travis Norman, 1968–

IN LONDON
Directors on the
Board of Advice

F. Larkworthy, 1875–1883[5]
A. J. Malcolm, 1875–1884
E. P. W. Miles, 1875–1887
Sir John Hall, 1875*†[6]

[1] v. p. 109, note 5.

[2] After taking his degree at Oxford, he returned to New Zealand to farm. He served in the 1914–18 War, being assistant adjutant-general.

[3] The son of Sir George Clifford (q.v.), he shared his father's interest in and success on the race course.

[4] He was President of the New Zealand Law Society from 1962 to 1968. He came to London as High Commissioner for New Zealand in 1968. He was appointed Governor-General designate of New Zealand in 1971.

[5] He was the London Manager of the Bank of New Zealand. J. L. Coster was, of course, the Manager of the same bank in Christchurch.

[6] An Englishman by birth, he had emigrated to Canterbury in the 1850s. He returned to England for a short period in 1873. With some intermissions he was to

VI. *Piako*, water colour by J. Spurling, 1926. (From a print in *Sail, the romance of the clipper ships*, by J. Spurling and Basil Lubbock, London, 1929, vol. ii, facing p. 29)

C. J. Johnston, 1875
Sir William Pearce, Bart., 1884–1887‡
John Lewis Coster, 1885
Sir Charles Clifford, Bart., 1886–1887‡[1]
James Brown Westray, 1887
Sir John Eldon Gorst, Q.C., 1887‡
Thomas Johnson, 1887

Sir John Eldon Gorst, Q.C., 1880–1894‡   *Chairmen of the*
Sir Edwyn Sandys Dawes, K.C.M.G., 1895–1903   *London Board*
William Charles Dawes, 1904–1920
Allan Hughes, 1920–1928
Charles John Cowan, 1929–1944
Thomas Francis Tallents, M.C., 1944–1947
Henry William Stewart Whitehouse, 1948–1952
Sir Frederic Evelyn Harmer, C.M.G., 1953–1965[2]
Charles Ambrose William Dawes, M.C., 1966–1969[3]
Henry Tetley Beazley, 1970–

Sir John Eldon Gorst, Q.C., 1888–1894‡   *Board of Directors*
Sir Charles Clifford, Bart., 1888–1892‡[4]
Thomas Johnson, 1888–1901
Sir William Pearce, Bart., 1888‡[5]
W. C. Pearce, 1888

---

serve in the New Zealand Parliament for 40 years and was Prime Minister from 1879 to 1882. He was knighted in 1882. He was one of those most responsible for the passing of the Female Franchise Bill in 1883.

[1] An early settler in the Wairarapa, he represented Wellington in the Parliament of 1853 and was elected Speaker. Although a Roman Catholic himself, his ambition was that all religions should have equal freedom in the new colony. His son (q.v.) and grandson (q.v.) both became members of the New Zealand Board.

[2] He later became a deputy-chairman of the P. & O. S.N. Co. and Chairman of the International Chamber of Shipping.

[3] He later became a deputy-chairman of the P. & O. S.N. Co.

[4] v. p. 111, note 10.

[5] On Sir William Pearce's death, on 18 December 1888, a Mr Richard Barnwell, one of his executors, became a Director; he was replaced at the meeting of 4 December 1889. His name does not appear, however, on the list of Directors in the Annual Report for 1889.

Thomas Russell, C.M.G., 1889–1893[1]
James Brown Westray, 1888–1905
Sir Edwyn Sandys Dawes, K.C.M.G., 1889–1903
Colonel Bethel Martin Dawes, 1889–1920
John Beaumont, 1894–1901
Murdoch MacIver, 1894–1910
Oliver Roper Strickland, 1900–1905[2]
A. C. Garrick, 1902–1903
John Studholme, 1902
William Charles Dawes, 1903–1920
Joseph Gould, 1904–1912
Warrington Laing, 1904–1923
George Tolman Haycraft, 1906–1937
Allan Hughes, 1912–1928
Alexander Michie, 1913–1932
Sir Thomas Bilbe Robinson, G.B.E., K.C.M.G., 1914–1938[3]
Charles John Cowan, 1920–1944
George Felix Harris, 1923–1939
Arnold Anderson Trinder, 1928–1940
Godfrey Holdsworth, M.C., 1932–1934
Edwyn Sandys Dawes, 1937–1947
Henry James Fosbery Mills, 1939–1959
Thomas Francis Tallents, M.C., 1939–1946
William Charles How, M.M., C.B.E., 1940–1959
Henry William Stewart Whitehouse, 1940–1952
Sydney James Brown, 1944–1952
Sir Frederic Evelyn Harmer, C.M.G, 1947–1965[4]
Claude Wilfred Payne, 1947–1953
William Lancelot Dawes, 1948–1963
Thomas James Breen, O.B.E., 1953–1961
Adam Denzil Marris, C.M.G., 1954–

[1] In New Zealand, he served in the government as Defence Minister and also Controller of Customs and Navigation Laws.

[2] He had been appointed the company's first London Manager in 1874.

[3] Born in England, he went out to Australia and became prominent in the commercial life of Queensland, where he was for a time Agent-General. He was Director of Meat Supplies for the allied armies, 1914–18.

[4] v. p. 113, note 2.

Charles Ambrose William Dawes, M.C., 1954–1969[1]
Francis William Spite, 1955–1964
Henry Tetley Beazley, 1957–
Matthew Robert Weeks, 1957–1963
Percy Thorneton Bowen, 1960–1961
Ronald Michael Thwaites, 1960–1969
Kenneth Macrae Campbell, M.B.E., 1962–1966
Leonard Kenneth Cooper, 1962–1967
Stanley Grant Fowler, M.B.E., 1962–
Leonard Cunliffe Birnage, 1964–
Thomas Sidney Marchington, D.S.C., 1965–1967
Robert Edward Stewart Whitehouse, 1965–
James Reginald Leggate, D.S.O., J.P., 1966–
John Vincent Downing, 1966–
Leslie Gwynn Sankey, 1967
Richard Borlase Adams, 1967–
Gray Hunter, 1968–
Ronald Francis Arthur Hosking, 1970–
Alan John Bott, 1970–

[1] v. p. 113, note 3.

Appendix 2

The derivations of the names of the company's sailing ships

For a colonial company, which was founded expressly as a national shipping line, it is easy to understand the choice of native Maori names for its ships.[1] The lines already established in the New Zealand trade in 1873, Shaw Savill's and the Albion Line, had not yet made use of any Maori names for their fleets. The former, however, was to adopt the practice in the 1880s (e.g. *Akaroa*) and the latter, which had already made use of the British named New Zealand ports (e.g. *Dunedin*) was, in the 1870s, also to make use of those with Maori names (e.g. *Oamaru*). The N.Z.S. Co. was generally to choose for its sailing ships the Maori names of rivers in the two Islands. Such names which had also either an important historical connection or a personal association for a member of the Board were particularly favoured.[2] An attempt seems to have been made to alternate between a South and a North Island name.

The information given below comprises first a topographical description then an account of the derivation and meaning of each name; finally, reasons are suggested for the choice of each of the 18 names of the company's sailing ships. The topographical information is generally extracted from *The New Zealand Guide* by Edward Stewart Dollimore, F.R.G.S. (Dunedin, 1957). The distances given are 'as the crow flies' with the exception of the lengths of rivers. The subject of Maori place-names often seems to be as amorphous as it is scholarly. No attempt has been made to collect here all the possible versions suggested by the various works of reference. Instead, a full quotation is given from *A Dictionary of Maori Place Names* by A. W. Reed (A. H. and A. W. Reed, Wellington, 1961). Thanks are due to the publishers of both these works for permission to quote from them. The personal and family connections of Board

---

[1] This subject is discussed in three most useful articles by C. B. Sharpe which appeared in the company's *Maori Club Magazine*, Nos. 10, 12 and 15, between 1959 and 1964.

[2] v. Appendix 1.

members with properties associated with the sailing ships' names
have mostly been traced through the Macdonald *Dictionary of Canterbury Biography* in the Museum in Christchurch.

River 65 miles long, in Taranaki Province. The town of the same   *Waitara*
name stands at the mouth of the river and is ten miles north-east of
New Plymouth. An area of Maori settlement from ancient times, it
was the centre of a land dispute between the Maoris and Europeans
in the 1850s. This culminated in the defeat of Wiremu Kingi at
Waitara in 1861.

Waitara: *wai*: water; *tara* (short for *taranga*): wide steps. River
crossed with wide steps. Turi forded it with great strides. Another
explanation is that it simply means mountain stream (*tara*: peak),
and another that a young man searched for his father by successive
throwings of his dart, *whai*: to follow; *tara*: dart.

The choice of *Waitara* for the company's first ship only seems ex-
plicable by the desire to find an unexceptionable name which was un-
connected with either the Christchurch founders or indeed any of
the other three main centres, whose interests the Canterbury men
were attempting to focus on the new 'national undertaking'.

River 120 miles long, in Southland Province. A small town of the   *Mataura*
same name stands on the river which flows into the Foveaux Strait
ten miles from Invercargill. There was a whaling station at the
mouth of the river in the early days.

Mataura: reddish, eddying water. The swamp water which drains
into the river is impregnated with oxide of iron.

The first ship having been named after a North Island river, this
choice was perhaps made in deference to the shareholders and potential shippers of Otago–Southland at this time being part of that
Province.

Corruption of either Rangitikei: a considerable river of the North   *Rangitiki*
Island, 115 miles long, which rises in the Kaimanawa mountains and
enters the South Taranaki Bight some 50 miles north of Wellington;

or Rangitaiki: a stream 95 miles long which for much of its course passes through the Urewera country. It flows into the Bay of Plenty seven miles west of Whakatane.

Rangitikei: *rangi*: sky or day; *tikei*: to stretch the legs. A day of striding out. It may also refer to a ford which was crossed by walking on tiptoes. Rangitaiki: *rangi*: chief; *tai*: tide; *ki*: full. A great river like a full tide.

This choice continued the alternation of North and South Island names. It is strange that the name should have been misspelt (although this has since occurred even with an English name – *Westmoreland* 1917–1942). Whichever the original inspiration, Rangitikei or Rangitaiki (the former seems the more likely), the name would have found favour with the Rhodes family who had property in both areas.

Waimea   Tributary of the Mataura river (q.v.) in Southland Province. The name is also found in Auckland, Nelson and Westland Provinces.

Waimea: several meanings have been given to the name: *wai*: water; *mea*: unimportant, forgotten. The stream with the forgotten name. *Mea* may be a contraction of *meha*: tasteless. The use of the name is widespread, and could mean insipid, tasteless, unimportant, lonely, unpalatable, etc.

Although it was probably either the tributary of the Mataura or the Nelson Province Waimea which was uppermost in mind in this choice, it was an auspicious name having connections with two other Provinces.

Rakaia   A large river of Canterbury rising in the Southern Alps and flowing south-eastwards across the Canterbury plains to enter the Canterbury Bight 25 miles south-west of Christchurch. The bridge across the river at the town of Rakaia is one mile long and reputedly the longest in New Zealand.

Rakaia: adorned. It is probably the South Island form of *rangaia*: to arrange in ranks, and refers to the need for strong men to stand in ranks to break the force of the current for the weaker ones when attempting to ford the river.

The first unequivocally Canterbury name to be chosen, and appropriately so for the first ship to be built specifically for the company, the name had particular associations with the Studholme and Rhodes families – the former having extensive properties on the river.

The principal river of the North Island and the longest (220 miles) *Waikato*
in New Zealand. It rises on the eastern side of Mt Ruapehu and flows through Lake Taupo on its way to the Tasman Sea 30 miles south of Auckland. Along part of its upper course it is known by the alternative name of Tongariro.
Waikato: *wai*: water; *kato*: to flow. Full flowing river.
An inevitable choice for a company pledged to the choice of Maori river names, Waikato was to have special associations for the Studholme family who were about to purchase a property bounded by the river.

A locality in the Bay of Islands in Auckland Province, and the site *Waitangi*
of early missionary endeavour. It takes its name from a river but is chiefly associated with the Treaty signed at the Residency on 6 February 1840, under which the Maoris ceded sovereignty to Queen Victoria. In earlier times, the Waitaki, a large river rising in the Southern Alps and for part of its course marking the boundary between Canterbury and Otago, was known also as the Waitangi (v. p. 105). Waitaki is in fact the South Island dialectal form of Waitangi.
Waitangi: *wai*: water; *tangi*: weeping or sounding. Noisy or weeping waters.
While its North Island historical associations make it one of the most famous of Maori names, it also appears in the South Island in connection with the Studholme family.

A borough and also a county in Canterbury Province, it lies almost *Waimate*
equidistant from Timaru and Oamaru. The name Waimate also occurs more than once in Auckland Province.

Waimate: *wai*: water; *mate*: stagnant. The original name in the South Island was Waimatemate, with the same meaning. Until floods came, the creeks became blocked up and there were many stagnant pools.

This choice completed the first quartet of new ships which were to be named after two North and two South Island rivers. Waimate Station in Canterbury was 'the sheet anchor of the Studholmes' land holdings' (Macdonald *op. cit.*) and in 1874 the family presented to the town of Waimate an area of 83 acres which was named Knottingley Park. Another Board member, J. T. Peacock, also owned property in Waimate.

Orari   A small river of Canterbury which flows into the Canterbury Bight about 12 miles north-east of Timaru. There is a township of Orari which stands to the south of the river.

Orari: the place of Rari. Literally, *o*: the place of; *rari*: a fish.

This was the first name to be chosen for the second series of new building; care was again apparently taken to spread the naming between the two Islands.

Otaki   A river which rises in the Tararua range and flows into the Taranaki Bight about 50 miles north-west of Wellington. The town of Otaki, which lies a few miles from the mouth of the river, is notable for its fine Maori church erected in 1846. The area is also associated with the great Maori overlord Te Rauparaha, who died there in 1849.

Otaki: *o*: the place of; *taki*: to stick in. The place where the staff was stuck in the ground by Hau, who was pursuing his wife.

This North Island name was evidently chosen to match the South Island *Orari*.

Hurunui   River, 90 miles long, of North Canterbury. It flows into Pegasus Bay about 50 miles north-east of Christchurch. There is a township of the same name which stands on the south side of the river.

Hurunui: *huru*: hair; *nui*: big. One explanation is that the name means flowing hair. It does have something of this appearance from the hills. It may have taken its name from the female dog, Hurunui, which Kupe was supposed to have left in charge of his discoveries. It may also refer to vegetation by the banks.

This name would have found favour with the Rhodes family, one of whose properties, St. Leonards, was bounded by the Hurunui river.

Waipa

The main tributary of the Waikato (q.v.). It rises on the western side of the Rangitoto range westward of Lake Taupo. It joins the Waikato river at Ngaruawahia. Hamilton stands five miles to the east of the Waipa river.

Waipa: *wai*: water; *pa*: fortified village. River by the *pa*.

New Zealand's longest river (Waikato q.v.) having already been chosen, it was natural that the largest tributary would soon also be favoured.

Wairoa

A large and complex river system of Hawke's Bay. The river is 50 miles long. The town of Wairoa, upstream from the mouth of the river, was at one time a minor port, the river being navigable for about 15 miles. The name is also found in Nelson and Auckland Provinces.

Wairoa: *wai*: water; *roa*: long. Usually long river, but in some places it means high waterfall, and in one place tall geyser.

The first four ships of the quintet built by Palmer's of Newcastle had already been divided in their naming equally between the two Islands. It was a happy choice for the fifth to be a name which though primarily associated with the North Island is also to be found in the South.

Opawa

The name of a small river in Marlborough Province. It is also the name of a suburb of Christchurch on the way to Lyttelton.

Opawa: the correct form of the name is *Opaawaho*, the place of the outer or seaward *pa* (village). This is the meaning of the name of Christchurch Opawa. The Opawa River in Marlborough is said to be *Opaoa*, smoky river, because the brown swamp water which poured into it gave it this appearance.

The earlier choices of names were generally associated with large rivers and often also with the properties of the farming members of the Board. Opawa river was a small one but the Christchurch suburb of that name was the home of some of the non-farming Directors including J. L. Coster and H. P. Murray-Aynsley.

Piako   A river 60 miles long in Auckland Province. It flows due north to the Firth of Thames and the Hauraki Gulf. There is a township of the same name near the river.

Piako: shrunk, or hollow. The name was brought from Hawaiki by the Tainui people.

This is another name associated with the Studholme family who had bought a property in the vicinity of the river in the 1860s.

Wanganui   A considerable river about 140 miles long in Wellington Province. Its main source is on the western flank of Mount Ngauruhoe. The river had been a canoe highway since ancient times. The town of Wanganui, which is also a small port, stands near the mouth of the river. The area was the site of Maori hostilities in the 1840s and again in the 1860s during the Hauhau uprisings.

Wanganui – Whanganui: *whanga*: harbour; *nui*, big. Great harbour. The pronunciation of Maoris of this district is rather different from those in other parts, especially because they substitute *w* for *wh*. For this reason the form Wanganui has become the accepted spelling.

A name chosen perhaps more as that of a great river than for any particular personal associations.

Pareora   A small river of South Canterbury 35 miles long. It enters the sea about seven miles south of Timaru. The township of Pareora is situated near the north bank of the river.

Pareora: life giving, or bountiful. The name may originally have been Pureora, a sacred rite performed for the recovery of the sick.

Levels Station in the vicinity of the Pareora had been acquired by the Rhodes family in the 1850s.

A river, 65 miles long, in Wellington Province. It rises near Waiouru *Turakina* and flows into the Taranaki Bight ten miles south-east of Wanganui and 15 miles north of the Rangitikei. The township of Turakina stands on the south side of the river.

Turakina: to be felled or thrown down. Hau, when pursuing his wife, named the stream because a tree was lying across it.

Except for its proximity to both the Wanganui and Rangitikei rivers, whose names of course had already been chosen, there seems no obvious reason for this choice for the last of the sailing ships.

75. *Mataura* at Port Chalmers. The coal-fired refrigerating machinery is responsible for the black smoke. (Turnbull Library)

76. 'Landing Australian frozen meat from Sydney, in the South West India Dock, London, from the s.s. *Catania*. Preserved in transit by Haslam's refrigerator, 1881.' The scene must have been almost identical in 1882 when *Mataura* discharged her first refrigerated cargo at the same dock. (*Illustrated London News*, 19 November 1881)

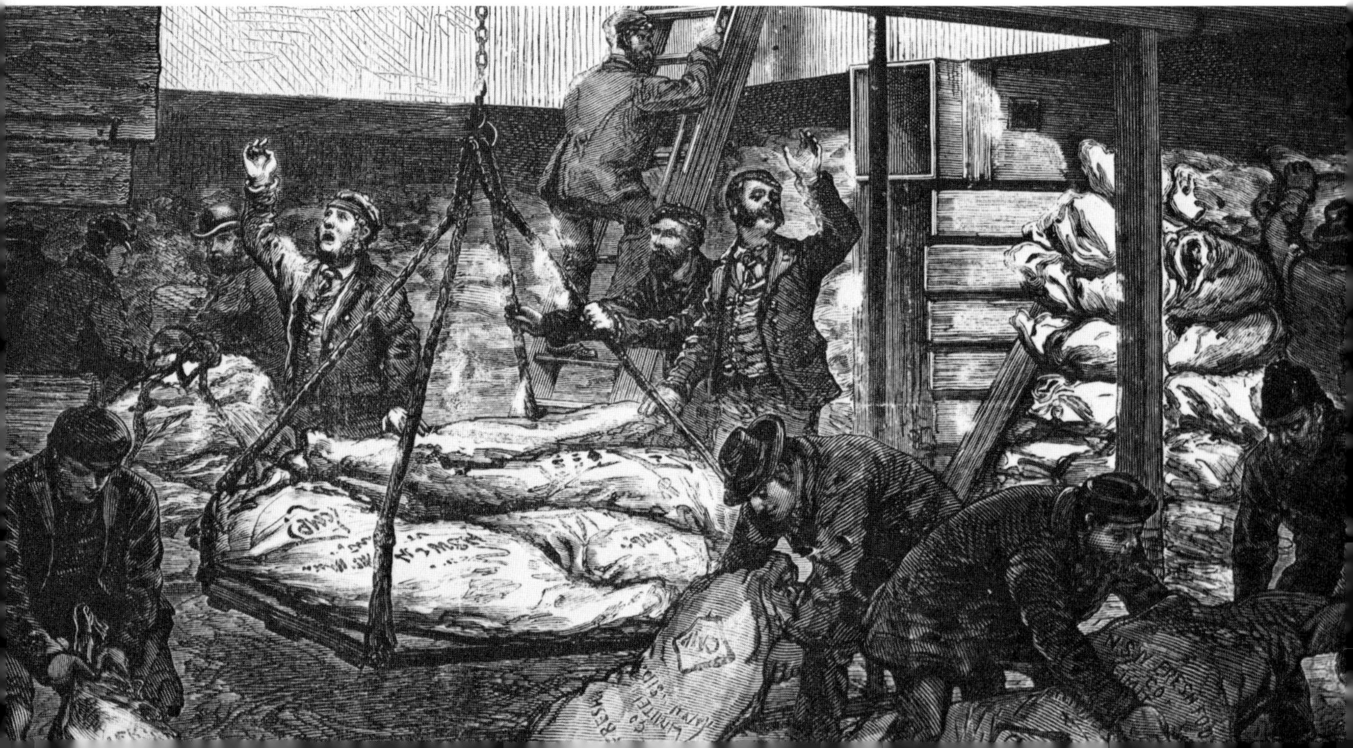

Appendix 3

The following account of *Mataura*'s first voyage with her newly in-stalled refrigerating machinery is extracted from *The Daily News* of 26 September 1882.[1] *Mataura* had been fitted with Haslam's patent dry air refrigerator earlier in the year. The first cargo of frozen meat from Australia using Haslam's system had been brought by the s.s. *Orient,* belonging to the Orient Line, less than a year previously, in October 1881. *Mataura* was the first ship fitted with this mach-inery to carry frozen cargo from New Zealand. The account is a model of reporting – factual yet vivid, interesting and somehow charged with excitement at the potential of this 'new experiment in food supply'.

Mataura's first voyage with refrigerated cargo, 1882

'A NEW EXPERIMENT IN FOOD SUPPLY – Amongst the latest arrivals in the West India Docks is the *Mataura*, sailing vessel, 1,600 tons bur-den, Captain Greenstreet, bringing a large cargo of fresh meat from New Zealand. This is the first voyage of the kind which has been made. Hitherto the large consignments of fresh meat from the Anti-podes have been made by fast-going steamers from Australia, New Zealand having hardly been thought of as a possible source of meat supply for London. Still less had it been contemplated to bring dead meat in the old-fashioned sailing vessels, which, besides taking a far longer time upon the journey, have not the resources of steam vessels for generating the necessary power for the refrigerating machines used for the preservation of the meat. The experiment, nevertheless, has proved perfectly successful, and is interesting as putting to the severest imaginable test the practical utility of the system of preserv-

[1] This is printed, together with many other newspaper reports on other machines, in a 28-page advertisement entitled 'Haslam's Patent Dry Air Refrigerators – 500 machines now at work'. This booklet was published by The Haslam Foundry and Engineering Co., Ltd., Derby, in about 1891. I am indebted to this company's suc-cessor, the Derby Pure Ice and Cold Storage Co., Ltd., for permission to quote from this publication and to reproduce some of its illustrations.

77. Sir Alfred Seale Haslam, Kt., J.P. He was the inventor of the patent dry air refrigerator. (From a photograph in the possession of the Derby Pure Ice and Cold Storage Co. Ltd.)

ing which is due to the ingenuity of Messrs Haslam and Co., of Derbyshire. The *Mataura* sailed from Dunedin at the beginning of last June, having on board over 4,000 carcases of sheep weighing from 90 to 160 pounds each, besides a quantity of poultry, fish, and provisions. For 102 days the vessel was driven slowly but surely by the "idle winds" towards home, and all this time in the hottest as well as the most temperate climates the cabin tables were well provided with the sheep, hares, rabbits and fish which were killed before leaving port. For no less than two months before arriving at the Western Islands, off the Continent of Africa, the thermometer, as may be seen from the neat and accurate log which was kept, stood at 84 deg. Fahrenheit in the shade, and 120 deg. in the sun. Nor was it only in respect of the supply of fresh meat that the officers and men were especially lucky. The refrigerating chambers were used for keeping all kinds of provisions, and thus the men were enabled under an equatorial sun to enjoy butter which was perfectly hard and cold, instead of being served up, as is generally the case, in the form of oil. The refrigerating apparatus is now too well known to bear a

minute description. It need only be said that it resulted from the
discovery of the apparently simple scientific fact that air when com-
pressed and afterwards expanded produces cold. In the present case
an engine of 70 indicated horse-power has been fitted up in the hold,
and with this it is possible to produce a temperature inside the refrigerating chambers of 60 to 70 deg. Fahrenheit below zero. It is
found, however, that a temperature but little below freezing point
is sufficient for practical purposes, and, as a matter of fact, the average
temperature during the journey was about 13 deg. below freezing.
Even at this point it was found possible to freeze liquids, including
sea-water, in a very short space of time. The difference between the
inner and outer temperature of the ship's hold is strikingly felt as
one plunges at a step from the hot engine-room into the great store-
house for the carcases of sheep. Here the beams, from which hang

78. Haslam's Cargo Machine 'for freezing meat, fish and other perishable food
on land or sea; for preserving with cold dry air all perishable food during a
long sea voyage: beef, mutton, game, fish, bacon, butter, cheese, eggs, milk and
fruit of all kinds.' (From cover page of *Haslam's Patent Dry Air Refrigerators –
500 machines now at work*)

innumerable carcases, enveloped each in a calico cover, are covered
with a thick hoar frost, which glitters in the sunlight as the door is
opened. Leaving a warm and sunny afternoon to plunge into these
Arctic caverns, one is surprised to see one's breath issuing forth in a
long white stream as on a very raw and misty morning. Everything
is frozen. The meat is as hard as iron, and here and there are some
hares and rabbits which would be no less difficult to carve, or some
water which has become as hard as the basin in which it stands. The
refrigerating process is kept up at an expenditure of little more than
25 cwt. of coal a day, the total consumption for the voyage having
been about 160 tons. This expense, added to the cost of carriage or
freight, and the insurance, which latter item, as in all new business
ventures, is indeed a rather serious one, does not increase the original
cost of the meat by so extravagant a sum as might be supposed. The
vastness of the consignment reduces the expenditure to comparatively
small proportions. Of course an article, as political economists say, is
worth what it will fetch in the market; and therefore calculations as
to cost are only interesting as having a bearing on the future of the
question. With regard to the present, it is not likely that the carcases
brought over by the *Mataura* will, any more than those already
brought over by the same process from Australia, fetch any sensation-
ally low prices. The meat is pronounced by those who have tasted it
to be of excellent quality. There are Southdowns and Leicesters, as
well as some sheep of a good mixed breed, and all are said to be
superior to Australian cattle. New Zealand, the England of the
Pacific, as it is sometimes called, possesses, as is well known, splendid
pasture lands and a mild climate, which is not subject to the changes
and droughts common to Australia. The sheep farms in the former
country, moreover, are situated nearer to the great ports, so that the
livestock have not to be driven two or three hundred miles to the
port, as is often the case in New South Wales and elsewhere. On the
other hand, New Zealand is one week farther from England than
Australia, so far as a sailing vessel is concerned, and this has to be
taken into consideration. The sheep which are now waiting to be
unloaded and sent to the London market were killed in the docks
at Dunedin just before the sailing of the *Mataura*. The price of
fresh mutton in that port is from about 2d per lb wholesale price to
about 2½d retail. With meat at sixteen and eighteen pence a pound

VII. 'When Sail beat Steam' – the sailing ship *Turakina* overhauling the steamship *Ruapehu* on 14 February 1895. Oil painting by Frank H. Mason, R.B.A. (London Office)

in London, it will be seen that a good margin is left for the expenses of the importation which is now shown to be perfectly practicable. There appears little reason to doubt therefore that a new source of food is opened up to Londoners, and time and enterprise will no doubt enable New Zealand meat to be sold here at a price at which not even the most careful of housewives could complain. Hares and rabbits, too, although they have as yet only been brought over on a very small scale, may possibly give rise to a great importing industry. They infest the cultivated lands in New Zealand, doing great damage to the standing crops, and the colonial farmers would be only too glad to get rid of them. The fish on board the *Mataura* include some very curious specimens, among them an albicore weighing 130 lbs, which was caught at the Equator. This monster, which resembles a small shark, will be offered by Captain Greenstreet to the British Museum.'

79. John Shipley Ellis, passenger on board *Waimate* in 1881. (In the possession of Mr Edward Ellis)

Appendix 4

The manuscripts of the following narrative, together with some of the illustrations and background material, have been very generously made available to me by Mr John Ellis and Mr Edward Ellis, respectively the son and grandson of J. S. Ellis. The principal source for the account is a retrospective diary entitled *My voyages round the world September 14th, 1881 to June 30th, 1882*. This has been collated with other notes and an essay entitled 'Days and Nights at Sea' which was written perhaps 50 years after the diary and which covers much the same ground. This account is further corroborated by a number of letters written by J. S. Ellis to his parents during the voyage and extracts from these have also been interpolated where appropriate.

An account of an outward passage in 1881 'aboard "Waimate", a clipper sailing ship belonging to The N.Z.S. Co., a good and liberal company', by John Shipley Ellis

J. S. Ellis was 17 years old when he embarked upon the *Waimate* for New Zealand, having been sent on a journey of convalescence around the world by his parents. He had just recovered from pneumonia which had developed from a cold caught, so the story goes, after his not unnatural refusal to wear his sister's outgrown overcoat at school in a Yorkshire winter! After spending several months in New Zealand young Ellis returned home in the *Sydenham*, a ship then on charter to The N.Z.S. Co., and entered the family business of Ellis and Everard Ltd., a general merchandise company. J. S. Ellis's parents made a wise decision in 1881 when they entrusted the restoration of their son's health to a long ocean voyage, for he was to live until 1951 – his eighty-seventh year.

Although the voyage described was a relatively uneventful one, it has seemed well worth while to print the complete account of it. Apart from Ellis's pleasing youthful enthusiasm for the new experiences of life on board a ship, the narrative gives a vivid picture of the routine as well as the extraordinary events of a voyage under sail – the livestock on board, the tending of the rigging, the labour of hoisting and trimming the sails, the pastimes during the voyage and the massive meat breakfasts!

14 IX 1881
South-West
India Dock –
London River

Went aboard the *Waimate,* a clipper sailing ship belonging to The New Zealand Shipping Co., a good and liberal company. She was and is a splendid full rigged ship of 1,153 tons register.[1]

As the ship moved out of the South-West India Dock, I said good-bye to Father and Douglas who had come to see me off, and turned to look around me. The ship was pretty well crowded with people who were going part way down the river to see their friends off.

As we got near the mouth of the dock where it goes into the river, we hauled alongside the quay to take on board two splendid horses, which were going to be our fellow passengers out to New Zealand. Each was put in a kind of horse box to be slung aboard, and of course they did not approve of it at all. They had a groom all to themselves and arrived in New Zealand in almost better condition than they came aboard. We had also aboard a lot of prize sheep and some prize bantams, and several very curious ducks nearly as large as geese, besides a lot of dogs, including one tiny toy Skye terrier, said to be the smallest in Great Britain. There were 65 passengers in all, 22 being saloon. My cabin-mate's name was R. E. Hall, a fellow a few months younger than I; we got on very well together throughout the voyage.

14 IX 1881
Gravesend

When we got outside the dockgates the dock-tug left us, and a larger one got the tow-rope and took us down as far as Gravesend where we brought up, the night having come on very foggy.

Late in the evening I went down to my berth with young Hall my cabin-mate; he had the lower bunk and got in without difficulty. I managed to scramble into mine, and then we both had a great struggle to get down between the sheets, for the stewards had tucked them down so tightly we could hardly get in, and when we did we seemed to have no room to turn round and kept knocking our knees against the bulkhead and bunkboard. It was not very long before I thought my bunk was quite wide enough for when the ship was knocking about, it was all I could do to jam myself tight in and stick there.

[1] This should be 1,157 tons.

I was wakened very early next morning by trampling etc., overhead, and for a little time could not make out where I had got to, but soon remembered. The ship was quite steady so I knew we were not at sea, and it looked very foggy through the porthole. Soon after, I got up and went on deck and found that we were still at anchor, the fog being very thick. At nine o'clock we had breakfast, and a very good one too – mutton chops, Irish stew, dry hash, rissoles, curry and rice, beef (for nearly the last time), broiled bones and all manner of other good things.

After breakfast we went on deck and began to take stock of each other and look at the ships that passed us each way, for the fog had cleared up by this time and we were waiting for the Captain, who had been obliged to go back to London on business.

At 12 o'clock we had a cold lunch of potted meats, cold beef and pork (sliced) and bread, cheese and butter; then after that we went on deck again. It was quite fine and bright and we could see Tilbury Fort and Gravesend quite well, as they were only about a mile off on either side.

At four o'clock we went down to dinner, and just then the Captain came aboard, the tug ranged alongside and off we went. Dinner was always a good meal; we had mutton, and pork, and tripe or braised mutton or ducks or fowls and on Sundays geese and very good pastry with currants, cherries, apricots etc., all preserved in the pies; grand plum puddings and mince pies about three times a week, and dessert on Sunday and Thursday. After dinner we again went on deck, but the fog began again to come on and we had to bring up for the night at the Nore.

When I got up next morning we were again progressing through the Downs – nearly a dead calm, and beautifully bright. We kept close to the coast and so had a splendid kind of panorama continually changing.

At Dover our pilot left us and the tug took us steadily on. We kept a little further out now but could still see the coast; it was still beautifully calm and bright and we all thoroughly enjoyed our-

15 IX 1881
Gravesend

The Nore

16 IX 1881
The Downs

Dover

selves. In the evening I and Hall, my cabin-mate, kept the first watch (till 12.0 p.m.) with the second mate – his name was Milward – and arranged that he should call us at 4.0 a.m. when he went on deck, which he did.

17 IX 1881
Isle of Wight

We hardly seemed to have turned in when I felt a hand shake my shoulder and – 'Turn out – it's four o'clock and the tug's going to cast off'. Up we both jumped and hurriedly dressing went out on to the main deck. There was a fresh breeze blowing and topsails and main topgallant sails were set. We could see St Catherine's Light on our starboard bow. The ship was lifting a bit but we managed to stand, in spite of our not having yet got our sea legs on.

The tug was still ahead of us, and we got under shelter from the fresh cold breeze and watched the sky gradually get lighter as the sun neared the horizon and the little clouds showed up red towards the east. Presently she slowed, and we all tackled on to the big hawser, and got the slack in, stamping it along the deck to the tune of 'What shall we do with the drunken sailor'. Then she cast off altogether and stopped, and as we passed her the fellows aboard her shouted 'Good-bye, pleasant voyage to you'. We cheered and waved our hands in reply, and turned our attention to the hawser again. After we had got it in we went on to the poop and watched the gradual change from dark to light as the day broke and the sailors up aloft making sail on her.

Then we turned in again to sleep till breakfast at nine, and we both did justice to it, and likewise to lunch – but then we began to feel ill, for the wind had freshened up and being a head one with a short choppy swell it made the ship pitch fearfully.

I don't remember much for the next few days though I was on deck all day in company with other sufferers. All this time we were 'close hauled', beating about against head gales in the mouth of the Channel. One day when I was feeling very ill my attention was called to a little grey patch of land which showed up on the watery grey horizon; on one of our tacks we had got within a few miles of The Lizard, and so we took our last glimpse of England for some months.

The Lizard

The next incident was a day or two after, when a small French barque came driving by. She had lost her foretopgallant mast and jibboom, and looked quite a wreck forward, with all her rigging hanging in bights. As she drove past she showed a board having chalked on it a request for latitude and longitude, which we gave her. Then she passed out of sight astern. 20 IX 1881

I was beginning to feel very weak with such continued sickness, although I was not so ill as several of them, when one morning I woke up and found that the ship was not jumping about and that I did 24 IX 1881

WEEKLY DIETARY SCALE

FOR

SECOND CLASS AND STEERAGE PASSENGERS.

ARTICLES.	Second Cabin.	Third Cabin.	ARTICLES.	Second Cabin.	Third Cabin.
Preserved Meats	2 lb.	1 lb.	Butter	½ lb.	6 oz.
Soup and Bouilli	½ lb.	—	Cheese	¼ lb.	—
Fish	¼ lb.	—	Raisins	¼ lb.	¼ lb.
Prime Ham	½ lb.	—	Currants	¼ lb.	¼ lb.
Prime Indian Beef	1 lb.	1½ lb.	Lime Juice	6 oz.	6 oz.
Mess Pork	1½ lb.	1½ lb.	Suet	6 oz.	6 oz.
Rice	1 lb.	1 lb.	Jam	¼ lb.	—
Flour	4¼ lb.	3 lb.	Pickles	⅛ pint	⅛ pint
Barley	½ lb.	—	Vinegar	⅛ pint	⅛ pint
Biscuit	4¼ lb.	3½ lb.	Treacle	½ lb.	—
Peas (Split)	½ pint	½ pint	Mustard	½ oz.	½ oz.
Oatmeal	½ pint	1 pint	Pepper	¼ oz.	¼ oz.
Preserved Milk	½ pint	—	Salt	2 oz.	2 oz.
Sugar (Raw)	½ lb.	1 lb.	Potatoes Fresh, ~~or~~	3½ lb.	2 lb.
Do. (Refined)	½ lb.	—	~~Do. (Preserved)~~	~~½ lb.~~	~~½ lb.~~
Tea	2 oz.	2 oz.	Water	21 qts.	21 qts.
Coffee	3 oz.	2 oz.			

For all Children and Infants an equivalent quantity of Sago, Flour, Rice, Raisins, Suet, and Sugar will be substituted for Salt Meat, if required.

Provisions of the best quality are put on board according to the above Scale for 22 weeks, together with an abundant supply of extra Stores, as Medical Comforts for Passengers generally.

The New Zealand Shipping Company, Limited,

84, BISHOPSGATE STREET WITHIN, E.C.

80. Weekly dietary scale of the company, 1879. (London Office)

The New Zealand Shipping Company, Limited.

WINE CARD.

To the STEWARD,

Please furnish me with 2 of Brandy

Name of Passenger, Alfred West

Date, May 13 1876

All Accounts to be settled Weekly.

81. Wine card of the company, 1876; actual size 2½″ × 3¾″. Reverse side is shown on p. 137 (London Office)

not feel ill, which pleased me much, I had a good breakfast, which made me feel much 'encouraged', and then went on deck and found that we had got a very light fair wind and a smooth sea. Now that I have fairly started, I must tell you that the Captain's name was Mosey,[1] first mate's Hardy, second mate's Milward, third mate's Moorhouse and three apprentices, Blanchard, Donald and Plunkett; [there were also a] steward and two under stewards, second class stewards, boatswain, carpenter, sailmaker, engineer (to work the condenser etc.), butcher, two cooks, four quartermasters (to steer) and about 20 A.B.'s and two boys. This fine weather continued for some time, until, in fact, we got well past the line. Our sickness gone, we all felt ourselves 'old hands', and looked over the side to see how fast she was going, squinted up aloft at the dog-vane, and then out to windward, with quite an air of knowing all about it.

Spanish Coast

While off the coast of Spain, although a great deal too far off to see anything of it, an eagle came off to us, but it did not settle. Another time an owl came off and stayed about us some time, settling on one of the masts as the night came on. He stayed all night, I think, but in the morning was gone.

[1] Captain Mosey had been master of *Orari*; he was to command *Waimate* for four voyages.

```
         ☸                    ☸
        ╔══════════════════════╗
             PRICE LIST
                 OF
         WINES, SPIRITS,
           MALT LIQUORS, &c.
              ─◆◆─
                              s.  d.
        Port  ...  ...  ...  per bottle 4  0
        Sherry ...  ...  ...      „    3  6
        Claret ...  ...  ...      „    2  6
        Champagne ...  ...        „    5  0
        Hock  ...  ...  ...       „    5  0
        Brandy   ...  ...  ...    „    4  6
        Rum  ...  ...  ...        „    3  0
        Geneva   ...  ...         „    3  0
        Whiskey   ...  ...        „    3  6
        Ale   (quarts) ...        „    1  0
         „    (pints)  ...        „    0  9
        Stout ...  ...  ...       „    1  0
        Lemonade,  Soda Water ⎫        0  6
           or Ginger Beer ... ⎰
        ╚══════════════════════╝
         ☸                    ☸
```

On 27 September we sighted a large French steamer lying-to, we supposed cleaning her machinery. That day I went aloft for the first time, and had to pay my footing for doing so; after this I went up aloft nearly every day, and larked about the yards and rigging and helped the apprentices when they were working, coiling up the ropes on deck, etc. For our amusements we used to play chess and draughts (chiefly the latter as the weather was too hot to think very much) but our chief game was Euchre, a card game much played in the Colonies; we never, all the voyage through, played for money, which was very nice.

27 IX 1881
Portuguese
Coast

One Sunday we tried to spear a dolphin, but the spear broke and the dolphin got away. The same evening we heard blackfish spouting quite near to the vessel.

2 X 1881

One afternoon, just after dinner, land was sighted. It turned out to be Porto Santo, and as the afternoon went on we passed it, and also Madeira and Deserta. We passed on the African side of these islands.

4 X 1881
Madeira
Canaries

The next land sighted was Palma, one of the Canaries, this was on October 5. On October 6, we had a concert – my part was a reading.

8 x 1881

On 8 October we had our first fire drill. When the Captain rang the bell we ran to our stations, swung the yards, and manned the boats and pumps. The women and children came aft, the steward brought up the gunpowder, the doctor (Dr Sorley) went to his cabin, which was the surgery, and altogether we had a good deal of fun out of it.

We now saw flying fish for the first time – they were not nearly so large as I had imagined, being about as large as a good sized herring. We did not see a single shark the whole voyage, and only one or two whales.

10 x 1881
Tropics
12 x 1881
San Antonio

We entered the Tropics on 10 October, and on 12 October sighted San Antonio, one of the Cape Verde's a long way off to the east of us.

12 x 1881
Cape Verde

As we are now in the track of vessels, I write this to send if possible. We are now well in the Tropics but I do not find it so terribly hot as I thought it would be. I am keeping up my log pretty regularly and intend to do so. We are all in pretty good health, though I have felt a little inconvenienced from the richness of the food in a hot climate. We passed a homeward-bound vessel today, but she did not see our signals. This ship is a very fast one – there are very few that can hold a candle to it for sailing. Our greatest daily run is 270 miles, our least 57. She is wonderfully steady under sail, and carries a lot of it too.

14 x 1881
Doldrums

On October 14, some of the passengers, but not me, started a school for the children, as they kicked up such a row. Our trend was now towards the South American coast, and we got into Doldrums north of the line, where it was very calm and the rain came down by bucketsful.

Ships have been in sight for the last two days but all of them outward bound. This morning however there are two homeward-bounds
quite close, and one other; we are nearing them and I expect shall
signal them – I hope to send this letter by one. It is very hot now as
we are getting quite near to the line. I had my hair cut the other day
by one of the quartermasters and feel much cooler now. We have
awnings rigged up or else we could not possibly sit on deck; where
it is not thus protected the pitch boils out of the seams.

After dodging about here (in the Doldrums) for some days we caught
the S.E. trades and crossed the line on October 22; we did not have
any of King Neptune's foolery – in fact he did not board us at all.
Being now well into the trades we had a nice steady seven knot
breeze, and on October 27 we were precisely under the sun, in Lat.
13.0 S. Long. 32.41 W.

October 29 (Saturday). A homeward-bound ahead will perhaps take
letters. We are in the S.E. trades going about seven knots. Splendidly
fine weather, altogether most enjoyable. Last Tuesday (October 25)
we had another concert in which I took a part – a comic reading. We
got into Tropics about 10 October and are now about 15° south of
the line. We have been rather long going this far, but still hope to
make a quick passage. I am writing this in a great hurry as the ship is
so near. We had a very wet Doldrums but now we have it very fine.
I must conclude – I hope you are all well; my love to all at home.
    The ship mentioned above was the *Sea King* homeward-bound for
San Francisco. We signalled her but were going too fast to stop for
letters.

The weather now got rapidly cooler, and on October 30 in the evening we passed between Trinidad and the Martin Vaz rocks; the same
night or early next morning we passed out of the Tropics. We very
soon began to put on all our warm clothes – we felt the change very
much, and all of us went in for chilblains extensively.

82. Captain Richard Mosey, Master of *Waimate* 1881–1884. (From *White Wings*, p. 266)

Gough Island

We lost the S.E. trades soon after leaving the Tropics, and shaped our course for Gough Island. I do not think we sighted it; we were becalmed for about half a day not far off it, when we saw some penguins. They seemed to work their feet like screw propellers, and went along at a great rate half under water; they were not nearly so big as I had imagined, though there may be a larger species than those we saw.

After leaving Gough Island we bore southward and eastward, direct for the south end of New Zealand, running nearly due east along the 47th parallel of Latitude, or as it is called 'running our Easting down'. We went some degrees to the southward of the Cape

Cape of
Good Hope

of Good Hope, and we felt it now pretty cold, and had a good deal more wind and bigger seas; indeed by the Cape you come across bigger seas than almost anywhere else.

On November 14 (Monday) we had a hard gale on the port quarter and on November 17, between the Cape and the Crozets, we had to heave to because the wind was due east, right against us.

Now, too, almost every night we could see the beautiful Southern Lights flashing away with splendid pure white streamers running up nearly to the zenith, or oftener, merely lying as a great bank of white light to the southward. Opinions were divided as to what it was. I maintained that it was caused by electricity, which I believe to be correct, and which seemed to be borne out by the Captain's and mate's statement that they had sometimes heard a crackling noise as the streamers rushed upwards. They said that it was the reflection of the sun's light off the ice at the South Pole, though how the light could crackle they did not explain.

We did not now sight any vessels; indeed it is very unusual to do so while running the Easting down. We passed to the nor'ard of the Crozets and Prince Edward Isles, getting along very quickly. We enjoyed it all in spite of the cold which, though not really much below 40° in the daytime, we all felt very much.

We used the fine weather to paint and clean the ship; I amused myself by painting the names and badges on the boats and lifebuoys, and helping to paint the boats themselves. We also helped the men scrape the varnished work about the ship, while other men were at work about the rigging, some tarring down, others filling fresh chafing mats on the standing rigging and reeving fresh running rigging, etc.

Whilst employed in this way we were surprised one morning to see a vessel ahead which we rapidly overhauled and passed in the afternoon. She proved to be a German barque ex America bound for Tasmania with kerosene and notions.[1] We soon left her astern, and did not see any more vessels till we sighted New Zealand.

[1] Miscellaneous wares.

No. 958

THE NEW ZEALAND SHIPPING COMPANY, LIMITED

84, BISHOPSGATE STREET   N Z S C   WITHIN, LONDON, E.C.

CABIN PASSENGERS' CONTRACT TICKET.

1.—A Contract Ticket in this form must be given to every Passenger engaging a Passage in a "Passenger Ship" from the United Kingdom to any place out of Europe, and not being within the Mediterranean Sea, under a Penalty not exceeding £50.

2.—Unless the Passengers are to have a free Table, the Victualling Scale for the Voyage must be appended to the Contract Ticket.

3.—All the Blanks must be correctly and legibly filled in, and the Ticket must be legibly signed with the Christian Names and Surname and Address in full of the party issuing the same.

4.—The Day of the Month on which the Ship is to sail must be inserted in Words, and not in Figures only

5.—When once issued, this Ticket must not be withdrawn from the Passenger, nor any Alteration or Erasure made in it, unless with his consent

Ship *Waimate* of *1124* Tons Register, to sail from LONDON for *Canterbury* on the *Thirteenth* day of *September* 1881

NAMES.	No. of Persons.	
	Adults above 12 Years.	Children 12 Years and under.
Mr Ellis		
		1
Total No. of Persons	*52. 10.*	

In consideration of the Sum of £ *45 : 10 : 0* I hereby agree with the Person named above that such Person shall be provided with First Class Cabin Passage (*exclusive of Wines, Beer, and Spirits*), in the above-mentioned Ship, to sail from the Port of LONDON to the Port of *Port Lyttelton* in NEW ZEALAND, with not less than Forty Cubical Feet of Luggage space for each Adult, and that such Person shall be victualled as First Class Cabin Passenger during the Voyage and the time of detention at any place before its termination; and I further engage to land the Person aforesaid, with *his* Luggage, at the last-mentioned Port, free of any charge beyond the Passage Money aforesaid; and I hereby acknowledge to have received the Sum of £ *22 : 10 : 0* in {part / full} Payment of such Passage Money.

£30 Balance   For O. M. Shelland   H. S. Inman   14/9/81

For OLIVER WALKER STRICKLAND

Signature *H. S. Inman*

LONDON, *23rd Sept* 1881

Deposit £ *22 : 10 : 6*

Balance £ *30 : 10 : 6* {To be paid at 84, Bishopsgate Street Within, London, E.C. three days prior to Embarkation.

Total... £ *45 : 0 : 0*
52 .. 10

NOTICE TO CABIN PASSENGERS.

1. If Cabin Passengers, through no default of their own, fail to obtain a Passage in the Ship, and on the Day named in this Contract Tickets, they may obtain Redress for Breach of Contract by summary process under the 73rd Section of the "Passengers' Act, 1855."

2. Cabin Passengers must produce on demand their Contract Ticket to the Government Emigration Officer under a penalty not exceeding £10. This Ticket should therefore be preserved and kept in readiness to be produced on board the ship.

N.B.—This Contract Ticket is exempt from Stamp Duty.

DUNN, COLLIN & Co., Shipping Printers, St. Mary Axe, E.C.

We usually had very fine winds, one day covering the enormous distance of 354 knots or nautical miles in the day, which as we were making East Longitude, would only be about 23 hours 30 minutes long. On several other days we made 260 or 270, and one 290 miles in the day.

27 XI 1881

When we got about level with Cape Leeuwin South Australia (but much to the south'ard), we had a very hard north-easterly gale with a tremendous head sea lasting three days, which made most of us, including myself, feel squeamish again, though not actually seasick.

9 XII 1881
Cape Leeuwin

After this we had very warm weather and light winds; the ship was all cleaned up and looked very nice. About the last thing to do was to fit new dog-vanes to the mastheads. I fixed the fore and mizzen, and the job took me a good long time, but it looked very nice when finished.

On the morning of December 14, 1881, the second mate woke me with the news that land was in sight to windward, and the ship *Canterbury* (Patrick Henderson Line) about a mile or mile and a half to leeward. I got up and went on deck; there was a strong beam wind, the ship was going about 12 knots, the *Canterbury* just level with us, and the Snares (an island to the south of New Zealand) some miles to windward.

14 XII 1881
Snares

South Island
New Zealand

We had an exciting race with the *Canterbury*, and for some hours went level, neither going ahead, but as we headed up the coast and brought before the beam she (the *Canterbury*) forged ahead, and by the afternoon was some way ahead and rather more ashore; but the wind falling light we were creeping up on her. When the night came on we lost her in the darkness, she running in to Port Chalmers (Dunedin).

About 11 o'clock (six bells) at night, all passengers but myself and Mr Coleman[1] being below, we were caught flat aback by a sudden flow of wind and began to go astern quite quickly. The Captain soon

---

[1] Another saloon passenger.

83. J. S. Ellis's passenger ticket, 1881 (In the possession of Mr Edward Ellis)

was on deck and after working hard for a long time we managed to get her round and went on. Luckily, it was a very smooth sea; if it had been rough we should have had our decks swept or lost our masts, or something of that sort. These sudden gusts and squalls make the New Zealand coast very dangerous. While going up the coast we were caught aback three times, and had to put the ship round each time.

15/16 XII 1881   We spent December 15–16 running up the coast, getting a beautiful view of the Southern Alps, the backbone of the Southern or Middle Island.

17 XII 1881
Banks
Peninsula
Akaroa Harbour

When I woke on December 17 I went on deck and found that we were becalmed off Banks Peninsula, Akaroa Harbour being not far off. We had breakfast today with the 'fiddles' off the tables for the first time since we left the English Channel. This proved premature, for we had to have them on again for lunch and dinner.

After lunch a light head wind sprang up which gradually strengthened, and we slowly beat round the Peninsula until just before dinner we sighted the pilot's boat. We soon had him ahead and besieged him and his crew for news, and soon learned that Lefroy was hanged and that President Garfield was dead.[1]

17 XII 1881
Outer Harbour

5.30 p.m.
Lyttelton

It now came on very squally, and we sailed in under fore and main upper tops'ls, and foretopmast stays'l only. We soon saw the lighthouse at the entrance of Lyttelton Harbour and across the intervening flat ground the white spire of Christchurch Cathedral. We rounded the Heads in a 'Southerly Buster', and soon dropped anchor in Lyttelton Harbour at about half past five in the evening. The Captain's command to the quartermaster to 'lash the wheel' seemed

[1] Lefroy had shot and murdered a Mr Gold on the Brighton Railway on 27 June 1881. He was arrested by Scotland Yard detectives on 8 July 1881 (*The Times*, 9 July 1881, p. 7). A report dated 28 November from Lewes gaol said he was to be executed the following day (*The Times*, 29 November 1881, p. 10). President Garfield of the USA had been shot in Washington in July 1881; he died on 19 September.

VIII. 'When Sail beat Steam' – the sailing ship *Turakina* overhauling the steamship *Ruapehu* on 14 February 1895. Oil painting by Charles Dixon, 1927. (Christchurch Boardroom)

very strange, and made me feel quite queer. Our outward voyage was over and we were soon to part company.

In about an hour a steam launch came off with the port doctor. They did not come off before because the doctor could not be found. Some few of the passengers went ashore but I preferred to wait until the vessel went into the Harbour, as I had grown far too fond of the ship to leave it in a hurry.

On Sunday the men amused themselves with fishing, catching a lot of very fine rock cod, and one elephant fish. It pulled like a horse having flippers instead of fins, and it had a trunk like an elephant's, four or five inches long.

18 XII 1881

Early on Monday morning the men were hard at work, sending down skysail, royal and topgallant yards, which made the ship look very bare aloft. The sails were unbent and stowed. About 12 o'clock the tug came out, and in an hour we were fast alongside the Gladstone Wharf. Not long afterwards I went ashore for a stroll.

19 XII 1881
Inner Harbour
Lyttelton

I do not quite know whether I told you that most of the organ in the Cathedral (in Christchurch) was brought out in the *Waimate*. I was often down at Port Lyttelton and aboard the *Waimate* during the first two or three weeks of my stay in New Zealand. One day they were hoisting part of this organ out of the main hatch when the hook of the gin up aloft that the chain from the steam winch went round to hoist the goods broke, and the gin, chain, package and all came rattling down the main hatch. I was sitting on the coaming that goes round the hatch, so was not very far from the chain when it fell. Luckily it struck no one or they would have been killed, but in its fall it struck and broke a lot of cast-iron waterpipes.

I went out several times rowing and sailing in the ship's jolly boat with the apprentices. On New Year's Eve they had a great to-do, firing cannon and rockets and burning blue lights. Of course, by this time all the passengers had cleared out, and so in fact had I, for I was living

31 XII 1881

in the Christchurch Temperance Hotel where I was very comfort-able.

19 1 1882   The *Waimate* sailed on the morning of the 19 (January). I saw her out into the stream on the 18; of course the men came on board drunk so as to feel happy. There were only very few passengers. I wish I was going back in her.

Appendix 5

The following figures have been summarised from a printed book entitled *Statistical Report of The N.Z.S. Co., Ltd., 30 November 1897*. The whole work runs to 36 pages, and covers, in great detail, all the operations of the company's sailing and steam ships.

Comparative averages of gross receipts from freight and passage money and of expenditure per voyage of the company's sailing ships 1890–1897

Year	1890/1	1891/2	1892/3	1893/4	1894/5	1895/6	1896/7
Number of voyages	15	12	11	9	10	4	4
	£	£	£	£	£	£	£
Freight and passage money[1]	7,067	6,233	4,858	4,355	4,029	4,952	5,464
Expenditure	£	£	£	£	£	£	£
Port charges	367	439	502	496	451	431	510
Labour (cargo expenses)	996	948	747	780	727	867	820
Victualling	434	458	448	387	394	440	395
Graving dock expenses	65	67	74	76	59	66	69
Cabin furnishings	26	25	22	29	32	24	50
Deck stores	384	339	289	233	225	215	276
Refrigerator stores	17	17	15	10	10	11	27
Deck repairs	199	189	201	108	211	149	302
Refrigerator and insulation repairs	32	41	24	13	16	40	127
Wages	1,101	1,131	1,132	1,078	958	1,087	1,226
Miscellaneous	87	84	73	64	83	67	105
Coal	123	137	126	109	127	88	222
Water	8	8	8	9	6	7	7
Insurance	206	204	226	224	179	182	164
Commission	..	..	54	55	2	3	1
Claims	—[2]	34	14	13	19	11	18
TOTAL	4,045	4,121	3,955	3,684	3,499	3,688	4,319
Average registered tonnage	1,046	1,050	1,027	1,066	1,045	1,157	1,145
Average time on voyages (days)	281	297	309	285	282	322	321

[1] By the 1890s almost all passengers travelled by the steam ships, so that passage money makes a very small contribution to the receipts shown above.

[2] The figure for claims for 1890/1 is not recorded.

84. *Opawa/Piako/Wanganui*:—Builder's plans: 1. rig; 2. profile, upper deck; 3. poop and quarter deck, midship section, lines plan and body plan.
The reduction in size of the original drawings for reproduction here has, of course, invalidated the scales given on some of the plans. (On permanent loan to the National Maritime Museum from Alexander Stephen Engineering Ltd.)

"OPAWA" "PIAKO" "WANGANUI"

Scale 1/16 Inch to a Foot

Alex. Stephen & Sons.
SHIPBUILDERS & ENGINEERS
GLASGOW
DRAWING Nº

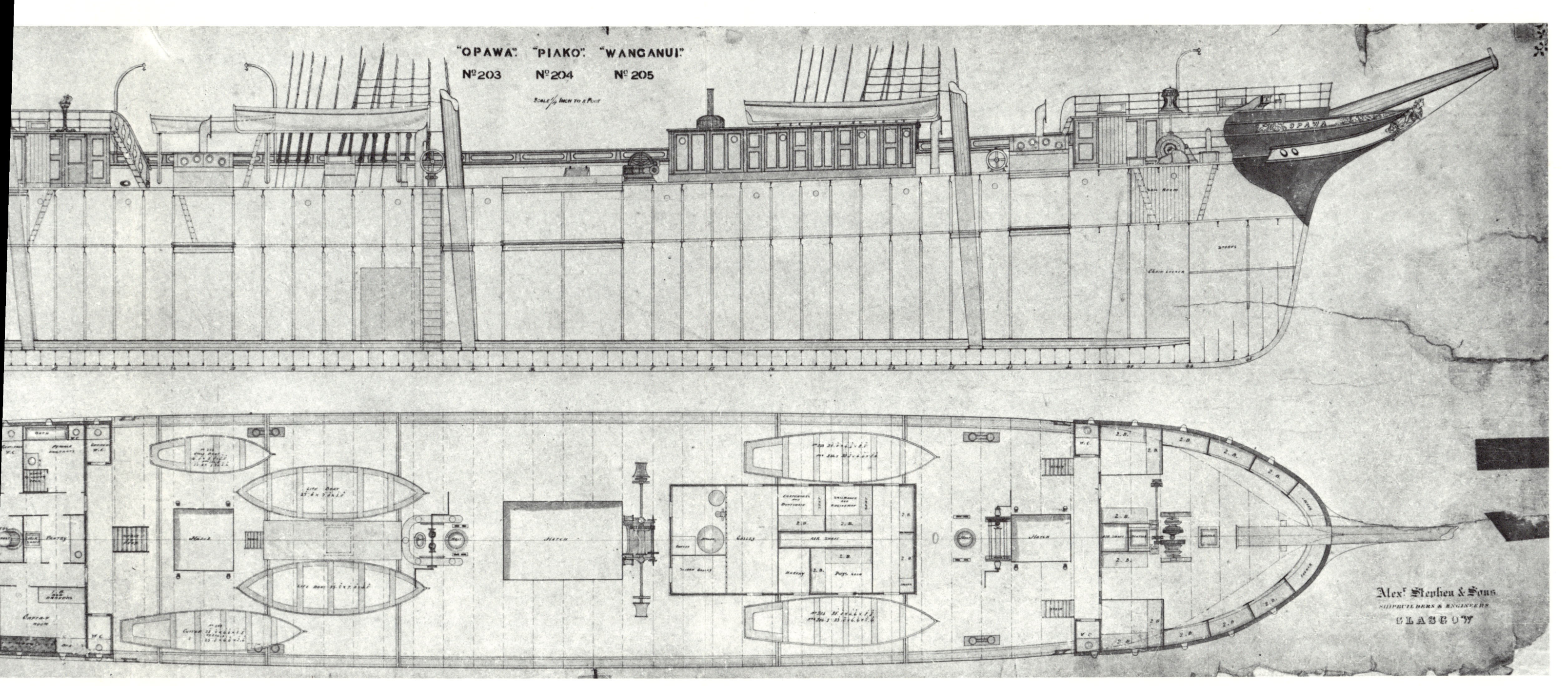

"OPAWA". "PIAKO". "WANGANUI".

No 203   No 204   No 205

Scale ¼ Inch to 8 Foot

Alexr Stephen & Sons
SHIPBUILDERS & ENGINEERS
GLASGOW

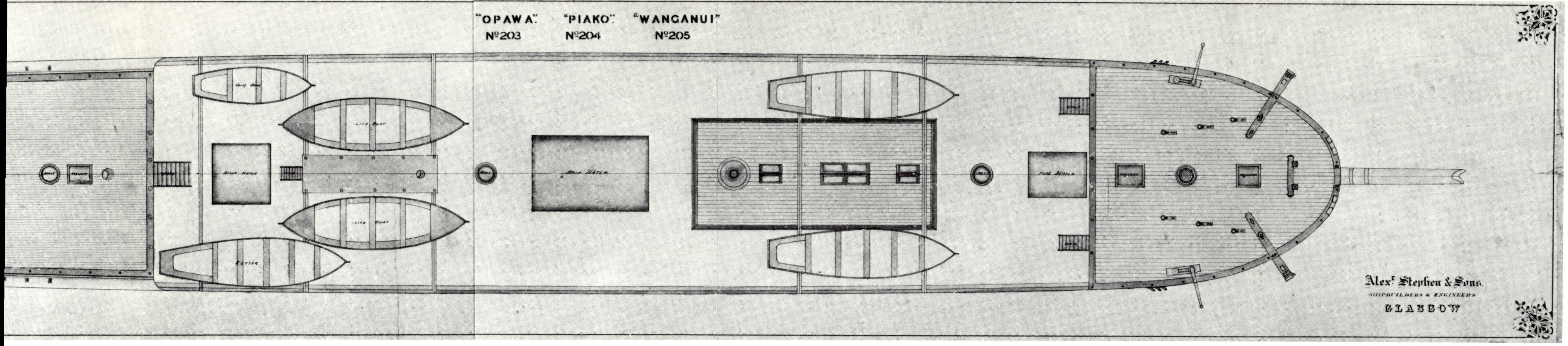

"OPAWA". "PIAKO". "WANGANUI".
Nᵒ203 Nᵒ204 Nᵒ205

Alexʳ Stephen & Sons,
SHIPBUILDERS & ENGINEERS
GLASGOW

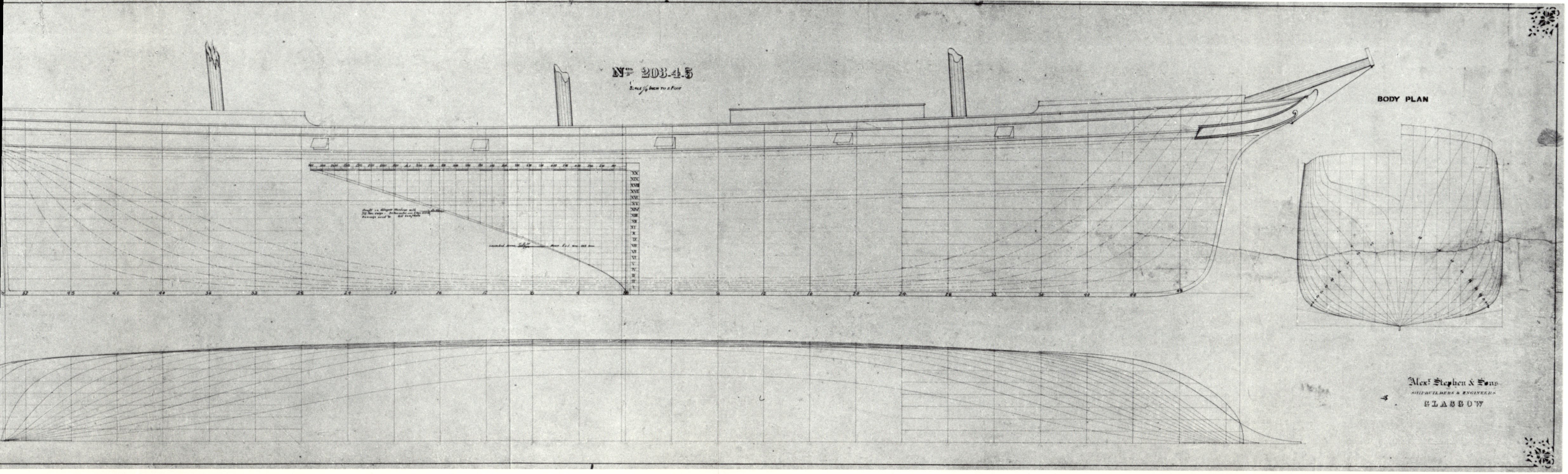

Nᵒ 203-4-5

BODY PLAN

Alexʳ Stephen & Sons,
SHIPBUILDERS & ENGINEERS
GLASGOW

Index

Note: The many items relating to The N.Z.S. Co. are each indexed under their respective letter. This has seemed more convenient than to have them all itemised under a very large entry for The N.Z.S. Co.

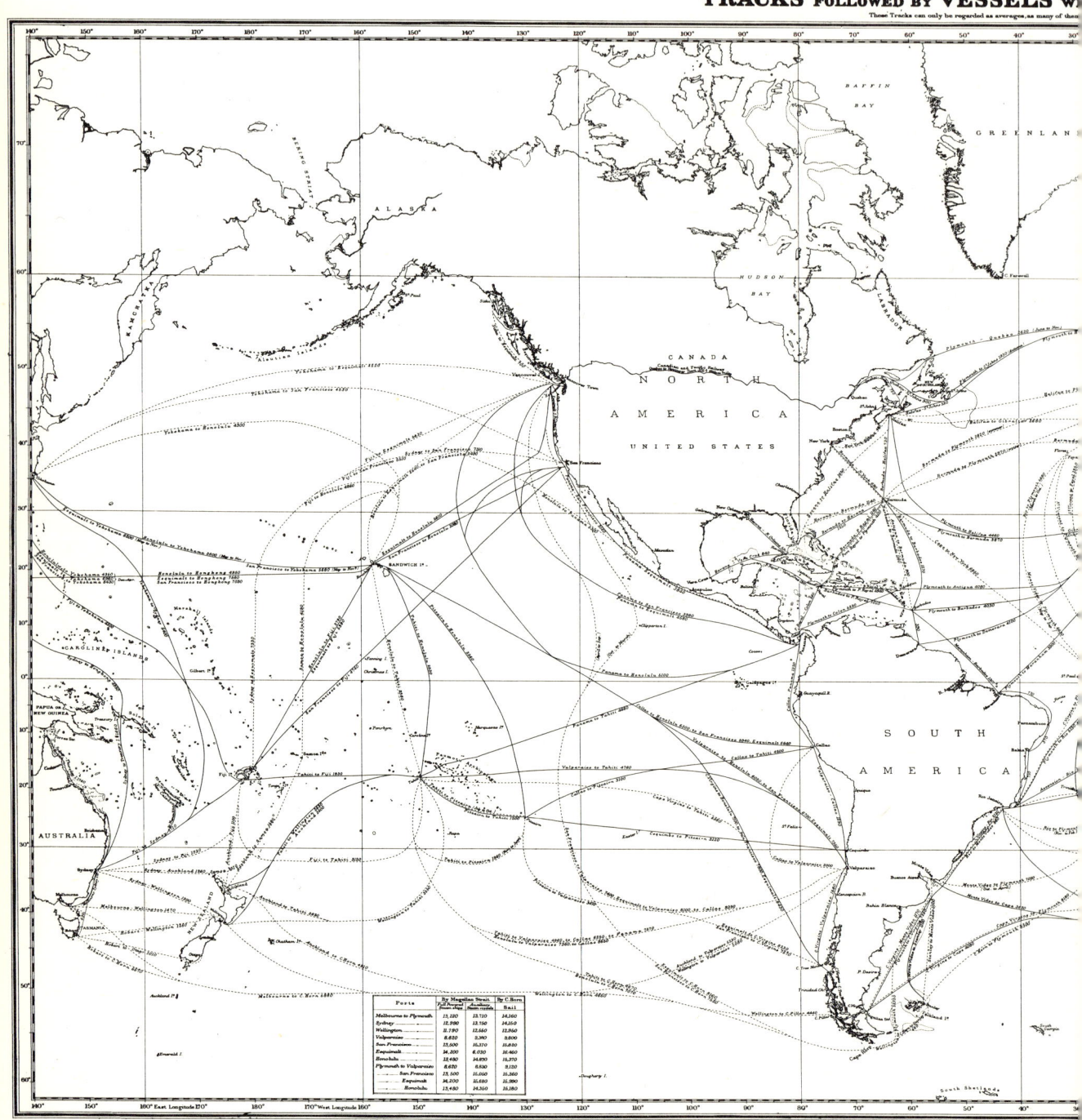